theatre & the city

Theatre &

Series Editors: Jen Harvie and Dan Rebellato

Published

Colette Conroy: *Theatre & the Body*
Jill Dolan: *Theatre & Sexuality*
Helen Freshwater: *Theatre & Audience*
Jen Harvie: *Theatre & The City*
Nadine Holdsworth: *Theatre & Nation*
Erin Hurley: *Theatre & Feeling*
Joe Kelleher: *Theatre & Politics*
Ric Knowles: *Theatre & Interculturalism*
Helen Nicholson: *Theatre & Education*
Lionel Pilkington: *Theatre & Ireland*
Paul Rae: *Theatre & Human Rights*
Dan Rebellato: *Theatre & Globalization*
Nicholas Ridout: *Theatre & Ethics*

Forthcoming

Susan Bennet: *Theatre & Museums*
Dominic Johnson: *Theatre & the Visual*
Caoime McAvinchey: *Theatre & Prison*
Bruce McConachie: *Theatre & Mind*
Juliet Rufford: *Theatre & Architecture*
Rebecca Schneider: *Theatre & History*

Theatre& Series
Series Standing Order
ISBN 978-0–230–20327–3

You can receive future titles in this series as they are published by placing a standing order. Please contact your bookseller or, in case of difficulty, write to us at the address below with your name and address, the title of the series and the ISBN quoted above.

Customer Services Department, Macmillan Distribution Ltd
Houndmills, Basingstoke, Hampshire RG21 6XS, England

theatre &
the city

Jen Harvie

palgrave
macmillan

First published 2009 by
PALGRAVE MACMILLAN

Palgrave Macmillan in the UK is an imprint of Macmillan Publishers Limited, registered in England, company number 785998, of Houndmills, Basingstoke, Hampshire RG21 6XS.

Palgrave Macmillan in the US is a division of St Martin's Press LLC, 175 Fifth Avenue, New York, NY 10010.

Palgrave Macmillan is the global academic imprint of the above companies and has companies and representatives throughout the world.

Palgrave® and Macmillan® are registered trademarks in the United States, the United Kingdom, Europe and other countries.

ISBN-13: 978-0-230-20522-2 paperback
ISBN-10: 0-230-20522-4 paperback

This book is printed on paper suitable for recycling and made from fully managed and sustained forest sources. Logging, pulping and manufacturing processes are expected to conform to the environmental regulations of the country of origin.

A catalogue record for this book is available from the British Library.

A catalog record for this book is available from the Library of Congress.

10 9 8 7 6 5 4 3
18 17 16 15 14 13

Printed and bound in China

For my sister, Juju Vail, with love

contents

series editors' preface

The theatre is everywhere, from entertainment districts to the fringes, from the rituals of government to the ceremony of the courtroom, from the spectacle of the sporting arena to the theatres of war. Across these many forms stretches a theatrical continuum through which cultures both assert and question themselves.

Theatre has been around for thousands of years, and the ways we study it have changed decisively. It's no longer enough to limit our attention to the canon of Western dramatic literature. Theatre has taken its place within a broad spectrum of performance, connecting it with the wider forces of ritual and revolt that thread through so many spheres of human culture. In turn, this has helped make connections across disciplines; over the past fifty years, theatre and performance have been deployed as key metaphors and practices with which to rethink gender, economics, war, language, the fine arts, culture and one's sense of self.

Theatre & is a long series of short books which hopes to capture the restless interdisciplinary energy of theatre and performance. Each book explores connections between theatre and some aspect of the wider world, asking how the theatre might illuminate the world and how the world might illuminate the theatre. Each book is written by a leading theatre scholar and represents the cutting edge of critical thinking in the discipline.

We have been mindful, however, that the philosophical and theoretical complexity of much contemporary academic writing can act as a barrier to a wider readership. A key aim for these books is that they should all be readable in one sitting by anyone with a curiosity about the subject. The books are challenging, pugnacious, visionary sometimes and, above all, clear. We hope you enjoy them.

Jen Harvie and Dan Rebellato

foreword

Woman: Part two was also their heartache for the city outside. They named it & renamed it every day despite the bitter cold. They called it remarkable city, alphabet city, alphabetti city, New Milan, and the Capital City of Britain.

Man: They sat up some nites & renamed it & their love grew as they named it: the city of spires, the Kentucky Fried City, the City of Elvis King, the exploding city, the city of joy.

And while they talked it rained like Ronald MacDonald outside.

Woman: That was the year the jet planes didn't fly anymore.

Man: That was the year they cancelled the Pope of the Year Pope contest.

Woman: That was the year that talks broke down in the Black City.

Man: That was the year that they shut the doors to the
Institute of Believing.

Forced Entertainment/Tim Etchells (text) *(Let the
Water Run Its Course) to the Sea That Made the
Promise*

Why city?

Because it is contested space.

Because it is used at the same time by many people,
sectors, factions, groups whose interests do not by any
means coincide.

Because it layers commerce, manufacture, leisure, the
political sphere – because it demands negotiation, compromise, co-operation, conflict, agreement in order to
function, in order to move.

Because if you look for even a moment at those things,
you see the ripples out to the bigger questions of our time –
the relationship between local and global, between cultures
nested in and around each other.

Because the city is a model of dynamic relativism, a
space where everything means more than one thing – a
nondescript doorway, invisible for some, is for others
the gate to a magical garden, a place of work, worship or
otherwise.

First time I was in Beirut, I was shocked to hear that there
were no traffic lights and no system of who has right of way.
Being used to things more orderly (raised in a place where

as few as two people waiting at a bus stop will try to form an orderly queue), I was wondering how the junctions could work. It's true that the driving in Beirut can be a little hair-raising sometimes (though not much worse than Brussels), and that the streets are littered in many places with the smashed glass of wing mirrors and tail lights, and that many cars, almost all perhaps, show some evidence of this quite everyday dodgem-cars trauma. But on the other hand the traffic works; it flows, stuttering for sure, but it flows. Another thing you realise is that the horn is a supremely versatile instrument, a sophisticated conversational device. The beep that says 'Go', the one that says 'What the fuck?', the beep that says 'Wait', or 'Watch out, I'm coming through', the beep–beep that's like a question. You need time to learn that language I guess, but even in a few days there you learn to love it, for its vitality, pragmatics and improvised negotiation.

Why city?

Because the populace is audience, or at least potential audience, and because they share the auditorium just like they share the city – in their differences, in their divisions of class, gender, race and otherwise. Because the tensions they have out there, the secrets they have out there, the journeys they go on, things they wish for or fear out there are the things you might well seek to amplify, uncover or remix on the stage. Because what we might call the temporary community of the auditorium (negotiated each night, triangulated off of the stage) reflects and refracts the temporary communities outside.

Because the city is a nexus of motorways, TV signals, suburbias, Internets, dreams, global currents and trickle-downs, a place where our desires wash up, are fed, disrupted, chained, dodged or neutered by what people call late capitalism.

Because the city contains small beauties, zones of possibility. Because it's thick with the ghosts of politics, old and current.

Because it reflects the life you must reflect and must reflect on and the life already reflected in you.

Because the city can trap you, nurture you, teach you, unravel you, unspeak you. Because you are just one among many here, and the dynamic of one in relation to many (conversation, dialogue, difference, the negotiation of public space) is what theatre emerges from and thrives on, what art must address and what cities must somehow contend with if they are to survive.

Tim Etchells is an artist and a writer based in the UK. He has worked in a wide variety of contexts, notably as the leader of the performance group Forced Entertainment and in collaboration with visual artists, choreographers, and photographers. His first novel – The Broken World *– was published in July 2008.*

theatre & the city

Introduction

Small Metal Objects at Stratford Station, East London

In autumn 2007, Back to Back theatre company from the city of Geelong (near Melbourne), Australia, brought their show *Small Metal Objects* to London, England, where I saw it as part of BITE, the annual Barbican International Theatre Event. Though presented by one of London's largest diverse arts complexes, *Small Metal Objects* was staged in neither of the Barbican Centre's two theatres but several miles east, in Stratford train and Underground station. The audience sat, wearing headphones, in specially installed seating overlooking the station's main entrance hall. Alongside the real ambient sounds of commuters rushing, ticket machines printing, turnstiles bleeping and trains drawing in and out, the headphones brought us a recorded music soundscape plus the voices of the show's four actors, who wore discreet microphones. The actors themselves played out their drama before our eyes but twenty to forty metres away on the station's entrance concourse and central stairway and ramp, initially camouflaged amid the surging and ebbing flow of real commuters.

The drama focused on the efforts of two wealthy and arrogant City executives to purchase illegal drugs for an imminent office party from two apparently suburban drug dealers. The first executive thinks the deal is secure because he has ample funds with which to pay, but dealer Gary refuses to go and collect the drugs because he won't leave his friend Steve, who simply will not move from the spot where he's standing. Increasingly anxious, the executive calls in his colleague Carolyn, and together they make more and more desperate attempts to close the deal; she eventually tries to persuade Steve by offering him oral sex. But Steve and Gary will literally not be moved, not by offers of money, nor by the false intimacy of free sex, nor by anything else the City executives might think desirable. Ultimately, Steve forgoes earning the price of the drugs in favour of staying with Gary and honouring the real, everyday intimacy of their friendship. The executives leave humiliated and empty-handed; Gary and Steve finally leave, no wealthier financially, but with their friendship confirmed.

Small Metal Objects showed that the city supports gross social and economic inequality through the uneven distribution of wealth and opportunity. But it also showed, within that unevenness, the potential the city offers its inhabitants to find human affinity, support and friendship. It asked why we value what we value. Clearly this related to friendship and money (including those small metal objects, coins). But it connected also to assumptions we might make hundreds of times a day about our fellow city-dwellers – those strangers we live with in our cosmopolitan cities – on the basis, for example, of whether they wear business suits or tracksuits, whether they move with assurance or are frozen by some secret fear, and whether they appear to feel socially entitled or are socially excluded. Back to Back Theatre's website notes that the company 'is driven by an ensemble of six actors considered to have intellectual disabilities', and *Small Metal Objects* 'explores how respect is withheld from outsiders – the disabled or unemployed – who society deems "unproductive"' (www.backtobacktheatre.com). The show drew the audience's attention to how we make such unconscious and literally superficial judgements through narrative but also through sensitising us to the uneven distribution of power often embedded in the dynamic relationship between those who look and those who are looked at. Inevitably, many passing commuters realised they were literally in the middle of a performance, cast as one of hundreds of unpaid, unwitting extras, and they looked back at us looking at them. Already eavesdropping through earphones on the private transactions of the drama's four characters, the audience could not fail to recognise our roles as voyeurs in the dramas of both *Small Metal Objects* and the everyday lives moving before us, nor could we fail to recognise the connections between the fictional and the real. *Small Metal Objects* was resonant in London, but it has also toured to acclaim globally, appearing in Singapore and in cities across Australia, the USA, Canada and Europe.

Why does the relationship between theatre and the city matter?

I open with *Small Metal Objects* because it exemplifies many of the reasons it is important to explore the relationship between theatre and the city. Simply put, exploring and understanding theatre in relation to the city can help us understand both better. Understanding the city, first, is immediately important as the world becomes predominantly urbanised: the United Nations Human Settlements Programme, UN-HABITAT, notes in its 2006/7 *State of the World's Cities* report that, since 2007, more than half of the world's population lives in cities (p. viii). Theatre can help us understand *how* we live in cities.

Small Metal Objects, for example, addressed whom the city is effectively for. It compared power-dressed executives with an apparent underclass consigned to a black-market economy in a context of grossly uneven economic and social opportunity. It asked what ideologies (or systems of belief) the city enforces, from neoliberal, self-interested capitalism to a climate of fear, in an age of anxiety about terrorism and of CCTV and other forms of surveillance (perhaps evoked in the pun on 'all metal objects', which airport security requires we empty from our pockets). And it asked where we think the city, its culture and its power are located – whether centrally, in the square-mile City of London proper, home to both the central financial district and the Barbican Centre, which some might see as elite, or on its East End margins in Stratford, where the show was staged and its ostensibly underclass characters made their home.

This is not the tourist destination Stratford-upon-Avon associated with Shakespeare. As part of the London Borough of Newham, this Stratford is one of the UK's poorest urban areas: in 2000/01 unemployment in Newham was 13.6 per cent, more than twice the national average of 5.4 per cent (Greater London Authority, *London Divided*, 2002, p. 111). In part to bring targeted investment, Stratford will host the 2012 London Olympics. It is also where one of London's most important 'alternative' theatres – the Theatre Royal, Stratford East – has long been based, staging a new kind of socialist working-class theatre under Joan Littlewood in the 1950s and explicitly addressing local black and Asian audiences in what is now one of the UK's most ethnically mixed areas: the 2001 Census indicates the local area then had a white population of less than 40 per cent, compared with London and English averages of roughly 70 and 90 per cent, respectively (Office for National Statistics, 2001 Census).

Small Metal Objects demonstrates that theatre and performance can help us understand city experience and some of the grounds on which we need to understand cities. Put most simply, cities are places where people live and work together in dense populations. But even such a simple definition raises key questions. What are the places like? What is the relationship between their private and public spaces, such as the train concourse or street, and between different parts of the city, such as London's Square Mile and Stratford? In a world increasingly connected by trade, travel and communications, what is the relationship of one city to others around the globe? Who are the people who live

in cities? We know urban dwellers are enormously var-
ied, coming from other cities, the countryside and abroad,
and encountering in the city hugely different conditions of
wealth and opportunity, but what does the experience of
city living make them? And how do people relate to each
other in such circumstances, where cities offer marvellous
opportunities – for example, for communication with so
many different people – but also enormous risks – such as
the risks of feeling alienated among so many strangers, and
of poverty, despite the city's riches? Do civic spaces produce civility or incivility? Finally, *how* do we live and work
in cities? People often live in cities for the work opportunities available there, but what work is this; how does it
structure our lives and affect our leisure? What work is it,
in particular, in an age when capitalism and consumerism
are becoming increasingly entrenched? Frankly, how do so
many of us negotiate living together in cities, the source, as
Richard Lehan puts it in *The City in Literature* (1998), 'of
both political order and ... social chaos' (p. 3)? So, to refine
the definition offered near the start of this paragraph, cities
are ever-changing geographical, architectural, political and
social structures where most people live and work densely
gathered in extremely complex social structures. Across
his career, social geographer David Harvey has argued
that they are better understood as urban process because
they are constantly changing (see, for example, *The Urban
Experience*, 1989).

Theatre, likewise, is an ever-changing material, aesthetic and social structure where many people gather to

participate – through work and leisure – in complex social activities; it is also usually located in cities. Theatre is therefore in some ways symptomatic of urban process, demonstrating the structures, social power dynamics, politics and economies also at work more broadly throughout the city. Theatre actually does more than *demonstrate* urban process, therefore: theatre *is a part of* urban process, producing urban experience and thereby producing the city itself. In some ways, how theatre does this is implicit and everyday: city people work in, make and go to the theatre; it *is* their urban experience. Alongside this, some theatre and performance aims explicitly to intervene in and change conventional urban process. *Small Metal Object*'s site-specificity, for example, aimed to challenge urban processes of social exclusion directly. Indeed, we might see theatre and performance as exceptional cultural practices through which to understand urban experience because of their long-standing literal centrality to urban life, their longevity as a set of urban cultural and labour practices, and the specific ways they both bring people together in live, shared encounters and offer people opportunities performatively to *influence* urban life.

There are at least three ways that theatre practices produce urban meaning: through their dramatic texts, material conditions and performative practices. The relationships between characters in plays about the city can tell us about changing urban social relations, as *Small Metal Objects* staged a conflict between characters with very disproportionate financial and social power. Aspects of theatre's material conditions – where it is located, what forms it takes, how it is staffed, how state policies affect it – can show us how material conditions structure urban experience: for example, which opportunities are most geographically, financially and otherwise accessible, for whom, in the city; how the city organises us as groups or individuals and reinforces or challenges social hierarchies; and how economic ideologies such as capitalism are embedded in everyday urban lives. And the opportunities afforded by performative theatre and performance – such as site-specific urban artists' walks, urban protests and performative interventions – increasingly appear to invite audiences actively to participate in making their theatre experience and indicate more broadly how we can interrogate and change how we perform ourselves in everyday urban life and who we are therefore able to be.

Critical strategies

My central aim is to explore how we can use an understanding of theatre in the city to make sense of and change social experiences in and of the city so that the many benefits of urban living are more widely shared. But I also aim to enhance understanding of theatre by reviewing and revising critical approaches to thinking about it, especially in relation to the city. My aim in this respect is to re-evaluate the two critical strategies I feel are predominantly and most influentially used within theatre and performance studies to explore the relationship between theatre and the city: cultural materialism and performative analysis. I have already begun to indicate what these strategies are and how they are practised, and later in the book I explain them in detail. But let it be enough for now to say that cultural materialism focuses on the material conditions of cultural practice and how these conditions affect – and particularly limit – the range of practices possible. For example, economic conditions might mean particularly popular plays are staged more frequently than unknown work, and the conditions of built theatre architectures might limit the range of audience/performance relationships available in a given theatre. Performative analysis argues that how we perform in everyday life constitutes us as who we are, reinforcing codes of behaviour to do with gender, class, age and other aspects of our identities. In the context of theatre and performance, it focuses on the ways they encourage us to perform – or discourage us from performing – particular identities. For example, gathering at theatres committed to a particular constituency can reinforce a sense of that group identity, or deliberately behaving contrary to cultural norms can challenge those norms, as when cyclists in Critical Mass temporarily dislodge the car from its dominance of the road.

Both cultural materialism and performative analysis have advantages and limits. Cultural materialist analysis risks suggesting that making socially progressive theatre verges on the impossible because theatre is always so constrained by its material conditions. Conversely, performative analysis can give the impression that theatre and performance are infinitely progressive, offering us unlimited opportunities to reinvent ourselves with unlimited agency. What's more, the two strategies are usually pursued separately. After exploring the values and limits of these two strategies, therefore, the book concludes by considering how we might combine them in order better to analyse and understand theatre and performance's complex meaning production, as well as the complexities, inequalities and apparent contradictions of our contemporary urban experience.

Structure and focus of the book

First, the book considers representations of city experience in drama. This section is deliberately brief, in part because textual analysis of drama is already widely available but, more importantly, to concentrate the book on my arguments about the limits of our current critical practices. The book thus turns to examining, second, the material conditions of theatre and how they affect the theatre's meanings for the city and, third, the performative opportunities that theatre and performance offer practitioners and audiences in the city. Having deployed principally a materialist analysis in the second section and a performative analysis in the third, I conclude by indicating why and how we might try to work those critical strategies together to realise the social, economic and artistic potentials of urban experience, to minimise their risks and to begin modelling ways in which theatre and its scholarship can best contribute to these aims. The book deliberately focuses on the present and recent past, and on the two cities which produce the most English-language theatre, London and New York.

City and texts

> In the West, of course, theater has always been intricately tied to the city and its forms of culture. From the Athenian civic and religious festivals, through the public and private theaters of the early modern period, its history parallels the progression(s) of Western urbanism.
>
> *Garner, 'Urban Landscapes,*
> *Theatrical Encounters', 2002, p. 95*

Drama has long narrated people's relation to the places where they are, what those places mean and what relationships they make possible. At historical times of extreme civic tension caused by enormous social change – such as rapid population growth, industrial and economic transformation, cataclysmic events such as war, or a shift from one dominant ideology to another – drama has repeatedly engaged with those tensions by addressing urban attitudes, relations, desires and disappointments. Through observing changing representations of the city in drama over time we can better understand how cities have changed and what this change means for those who live and work in the city. In this section, I look at the drama from a series of points in Western history to see how it represents its contemporary city's social transitions and tensions, particularly in relation to the Western city's developing market economy.

In ancient Greece of the sixth to fourth centuries BCE, governance was organised largely by city-state or *polis* – the quintessential example being Athens. And it explicitly pursued ideal, utopian statehood supposedly democratically, with power shared among the people, or *demos*, though actually only shared by the state-recognised citizens – adult males, and not slaves, foreigners, women or children. The period's drama staged the shaping of civic identity through the rise and decline of this form of democracy in important ways. Plays were often set in public civic spaces; for example, in Sophocles' famous tragedy *Oedipus the King* (Athens, *c*.429 BCE), the open space in front of Oedipus' palace. And they were populated by rulers and citizens, the latter frequently making up the chorus and calmly claiming power through both narrative and the theatrical effect of their unified multiple voices and bodies. In this play, Oedipus must recognise that the transgressions he inadvertently committed by killing the man he did not know was his father and marrying the woman he did not know was his mother have brought a curse on his city and citizens. To relieve the curse, Oedipus blinds himself and exiles himself from the city; the drama stages a purifying narrative in which the city is symbolically purged and renewed. What's more, the drama was produced at a civic theatre festival – Athens' City Dionysia – in a theatre acknowledged as an important civic space in the city's geographical and social landscape, and the festival would have been attended by many of the citizens of the city plus some of those considered non-citizens as well. The drama therefore staged subtly competing narratives of the city, representing a tension between conceiving the city as purged, progressive and democratic and seeing it as somewhat regressive and oligarchic – controlled by the elite few, not the many.

This tension between the supposed aspirations of the ancient Greek city-state to realise democratic greatness and its failures fully to do is visible too in the period's comedy. Aristophanes' famous *Birds* (Athens, 414 BCE) satirically represents leaders' fantasies of utopianism as deluded and self-interested. The play's self-appointed leaders imagine a new species of human-birds founding an avian-ocracy in a utopia called Cloud Cuckoo Land – a phrase so loaded with delusions of grandeur it has come all the way down to current usage, as for example in Radiohead's 2001 song 'Like Spinning Plates'.

Medieval theatre throughout Europe was dominated by Christian religious dramas generally staged so that the audience had to move around among various scenes (called pageants) set out on a path of stations in a church or, when outside, on a succession of temporary stages rigged on wagons. The stations or wagons represented various scenarios in a religious drama that often followed the arc of a biblical narrative, starting with Creation and ending with Doomsday but focusing on the Passion (Christ's life, death and rebirth). These play cycles were staged from the late fourteenth century until the late sixteenth in such English cities as York, Chester and Coventry in order, on the face of it, to give thanks for good fortune and to celebrate the glory of God; they staged a city's religious piety and worthiness. But it could also be argued that they staged mercantile opportunism, functioning as tourist attractions for city residents and

visitors, bringing business to the municipality and honouring the city as well as God (Harris, 'Medieval Theatre in
Europe', 2003, p. 829; King, *The York Mystery Cycle and the
Worship of the City*, 2006, p. 5). They also displayed the
wealth and – like advertisements – skills of the city's business organisations, or guilds, that staged the cycles' individual plays. Select notable plays in the York Cycle, for
example, were famously sponsored by the Mercers and the
Tilethatchers guilds (Davidson, 'The York Cycle', 1992,
p. 925). These cycles acknowledged the importance of reli-
gion and worship, but they simultaneously indicated the
importance of other principles of social organisation such as
the city, the guilds and the market.

The importance of the city and the market increased
exponentially throughout the late sixteenth century and into
the seventeenth in Europe, a change vividly illustrated by
Europe's fastest-growing city of the period, London. London's
1570 population of approximately 100,000 doubled by 1600,
doubled again to 400,000 by 1650, and carried on growing
until, by 1700, London equalled Constantinople in population, and the two ranked as Europe's largest cities (Finlay
and Shearer, 'Population Growth and Suburban Expansion',
1986, cited in Stock and Zwierlein, 'Introduction: "Our
Scene Is London ..."', 2004, p. 5; Orlin, 'Introduction',
2000, p. 3). Rapid growth produced enormous social change.
Urban populations grew more mixed through immigra-
tion from the countryside and abroad. Structures formerly
relied on to organise urban life – such as the guilds, but also
other systems of patronage and indeed the authority of the

Crown and the Church – had to find new ways to accommodate changed contexts. Capitalism was quickly displacing feudalism as the dominant economic system; women were gaining power; multicultural populations were diversifying social practices (of dress, diet and so on); the Protestant Reformation was eradicating Catholic festivals in ways that opened the door for theatre itself to become a more important site of community gathering, self-fashioning and spectacle; and a decline in the Church's traditional rural power coincidentally secularised drama and theatre.

In this context, from about 1590 to 1630, a genre of drama arose that was subsequently named city or citizen comedy. Famous examples, all first produced in London, include *Eastward Ho* (1605) by George Chapman, Ben Jonson and John Marston; *A Chaste Maid in Cheapside* (1613) by Thomas Middleton; and *Bartholmew Fair* (1614) and *The Devil Is an Ass* (1616), both by Ben Jonson. Set in London, filled with recognisable details of real locations and peopled with characters familiar from everyday life – lawyers, lenders, traders, craftsmen, apprentices, prostitutes, servants and criminals – city comedies explored contemporary changes to the social order and especially to socio-economic mobility. They broadly satirised both mercantile and puritan values by staging puritan ethics in conflict with financial opportunism, and they often concluded with a bourgeoisie triumphant over both their class superiors and upstart social climbers. City comedy was self-reflexive in staging savvy urban citizens who recognised new possibilities to self-fashion and re-create themselves at a time of enormous social change. It was also self-reflexive in acknowledging theatre's dependence as an industry on the many new consumers created by London's changing patterns of commerce, which increasingly disregarded old class discriminations to focus instead on the fiscal bottom line: did the consumer – wealthy or poor, aristocratic gentry or emerging merchant class, male or female – simply have enough money to purchase admission to the theatre? *Bartholmew Fair* indicates the ambivalence of Jonson's age to this market expansion/democratisation, which was recognised as being, at once, fiscally necessary but, for many, enduringly socially repugnant. The play begins with a book-maker and scrivener laying out the terms by which Jonson presents the play: he permits each audience member to judge it, but only 'to the value of his place', be it as little as 'six penn'orth' or as much as 'half a crown', 'provided always his place get not above his wit' (Induction, ll. 80–83). As the theatre replaced the Catholic religious festival as a key site of communal civic gathering in an increasingly secular age, it replaced the focus of Catholicism not so much with the royally mandated Protestantism but with the perhaps now triumphant ideology of capitalism. Importantly, however, it did this with humour, not so much selling out to this rapacious new ideology as shrewdly buying into it.

Following the seventeenth-century closing and reopening of the theatres in England, Restoration comedies picked up city comedies' use of the city as a ripe context for social observation, satire and celebration. William Wycherley's *The Country Wife* (Theatre Royal, Drury Lane, London,

1675) stages the sexual exploits of a London libertine who spreads a rumour that he is impotent to gain un-chaperoned access to women of virtuous reputation. The play celebrates the wit and ultimate superiority of the knowing, established urbanite compared with the naivety of a country-bumpkin, incoming, aspiring entrepreneurial class, while also subtly satirising the libertine's rapacious lust. John Vanbrugh's *The Relapse* (Theatre Royal, Drury Lane, London, 1696) shows a reformed urban rake – who has apparently been subdued in rural domestic bliss – quickly reverting to profligacy when confronted with the delights offered by the fashionable metropolis. The city is morally dangerous but, for many, irresistibly seductive; Judith R. Walkowitz captures this point in relation to the nineteenth century in the title of her 1992 book *City of Dreadful Delight*.

In the mid- to late nineteenth century, the city is adapted to the good-versus-evil terms of melodrama and peopled by the hard-working and virtuous, but also by ruthless criminals. The good – often naive incomers to the city – invariably triumph, but only after they have been sorely tested by urban criminals' extraordinary greed and duplicity. In Tom Taylor's *The Ticket-of-Leave Man* (Olympic Theatre, London, 1863), innocent Lancashire lad Robert Brierly seeks his fortune in the metropolis of London, is seduced by alcohol, falls prey to criminals and is imprisoned for three years. Bailed on a 'ticket-of-leave' (like Jean Valjean at the beginning of *Les Misérables* [Barbican, London, 1985]), Brierly attempts to lead a reformed life but is repeatedly thwarted by his erstwhile criminal associates. By aligning himself with the good offices of the law to collaborate with an undercover police officer, Brierly sees those former associates arrested and is recognised himself as a good man. In Dion Boucicault's *The Poor of New York* (Wallack's Theatre, New York, 1857), the honest (and class-privileged) Captain Fairweather lodges his fortune with the dishonest banker Bloodgood. Realising his money is lost, Fairweather dies, and his family fall into penury; Bloodgood, meanwhile, grows rich. Twenty years later, Bloodgood is finally arrested, though he is forgiven by the good Fairweathers, whose wealth is restored. As Bruce McConachie notes in *Melodramatic Formations* (1992), the play was frequently adapted to different cities of production throughout the late nineteenth century, becoming *The Streets of Philadelphia*, *The Rich and Poor of Boston*, *The Poor of Liverpool* and *The Streets of London*, which indicates how this tale of urban conflict – arising from differences of class, wealth and goodness – was felt to resonate in other cities far beyond New York (p. 211).

This global resonance of urban social conflict is increasingly emphasised in late-twentieth-century drama. The English writer Caryl Churchill starts her notoriously successful 1987 play *Serious Money* with an excerpt from Thomas Shadwell's Restoration comedy *The Volunteers, or The Stockjobbers* (1692). In the excerpt, seventeenth-century characters discuss buying shares in various inventions and entrepreneurial schemes – including a plan to bring Chinese performers to England. The character Hackwell repeatedly stresses that it does not matter whether any of the inventions or shows is actually ever produced or even purchased because there is money to be made simply in buying and selling stocks in speculation on an expanding global market. It is, he implies, the individual's right in an unregulated, liberal economy to make money playing the market this way. Shadwell and Churchill identify here a key principle that Karl Marx elaborates on in his monumental *Capital* (volume 1 of 3 published in 1867). This is the point that although financial value has historically been attributed to goods/commodities or services (including the labour of producing goods), as modes of production and funding production have 'developed', value has been increasingly alienated – or distanced – from the goods and workers in production themselves. Those privileged few who deal in capital speculation – or finance capital – can end up making the most money, and those who actually labour to produce the goods can end up losing out. The unregulated liberal economy, which supports the freedom of the individual (capitalist) to deploy his capital in his own best interests, may sometimes benefit wider society – for example, if Hackwell actually brings interesting international performance to a local audience – but it will also harm society by forcing the majority into exploitative and alienating labour. This economy is unregulated because government does not interfere with – or regulate – it to ensure it provides the best outcome for all, despite the fact that ensuring the best outcome for all citizens might very well be seen as a government's principal responsibility.

Churchill's play goes on to focus on a handful of international financial traders at a peak of neoliberal capitalist

excess in London and New York in the 1980s, an era dominated on both sides of the Atlantic by extensive reductions
in government regulation of economic markets in the
context of Ronald Reagan's Reaganomics and Margaret
Thatcher's monetarism. Thatcher defended her endorsement of deregulation in the infamous assertion made in an
interview with Douglas Keay for *Women's Own* magazine in
1987 that '[t]here is no such thing as society', a claim that
defended the right of every-man-for-himself to pursue his
own best interests, regardless of their wider social effects.
Though the play never explicitly returns to Shadwell's
The Volunteers, Churchill maintains a resonance between
the seventeenth century (and its liberalism) and the 1980s
(and the decade's resurgent, or neo-, liberalism), formally
by writing all her contemporary dialogue in loose rhym-
ing verse, and through content by following the lives of
1980s financial speculators. In the 1980s, we see again the
urban libertine's self-indulgent rapacious greed: one character says that 'sexy greedy *is* the late eighties' (p. 287).
We also see gross corruption, including how the wealth of
these urban traders in the North and West depends on the
exploitation of distant labourers in the South and on the
traders' own constant disavowal of this exploitation. The
banker Zackerman claims, 'Pictures of starving babies are
misleading and patronising. / Because there's plenty of rich
people in those countries, it's just the masses that's poor,
and Jacinta Condor flew into London and was quite enter-
prising' (p. 255). For her part, the Peruvian businesswoman
Jacinta Condor acknowledges that international markets

exploit her fellow citizens through trade in cocaine, a trade publicly condemned by governments in both Peru and the USA but financially relied on by the Peruvian government and demanded by the US market. 'Who likes a coke buzz?' she asks rhetorically, responding immediately, 'America does. / They stop using it, we won't grow it' (p. 262). The play offers a critique of the exploitations of international neoliberal market forces, showing how demand by the wealthy acting in their own self-interest makes the poor supply, even when to do so is ultimately self-destructive for the poor.

At the same time, *Serious Money* also engages with some of the social benefits of global trade. It demonstrates, for example, that although the worlds of financial speculation are snobbish and sexist, their liberalism – their commitment to allowing individuals to act in their own self-interest – creates opportunities for increased social mobility across former class and gender divides. The play shows trading floors as thrilling places to work and more than grants a heady poetry to their exuberant language: written almost entirely in verse, the play is punctuated by songs and repeatedly runs overlapping dialogues – for example, on trading and flirting – that demand artfully precise performance. As Linda Kintz observes in 'Performing Capital in Caryl Churchill's *Serious Money*' (1999), 'both the form and the content of the play celebrate as they critique the social and economic mechanism of late capitalism' (p. 251). *Serious Money* was so popular with the City traders it satirised that it transferred to the West End, and debate reigned about whether the play and its production ultimately critiqued or celebrated capitalist excess. As in the Restoration's city comedies, Churchill's play staged a tension between the attractions of self-interested, hedonistic indulgence afforded by the city and its liberal markets and the moral responsibility to others that cities can make visible by placing the wealthy next to the poor but that global markets obscure by erasing face-to-face contact. As social geographer Doreen Massey notes in *World City* (2007), 'Cities are central to neoliberal globalisation' (p. 9), which accounts for many of their economic attractions but also, because '[n]eoliberalism develops unevenly' (p. 18), for global economic inequality.

As these examples indicate, across history, drama has articulated the changing conditions of urban life, be those changes social, material, structural, religious, economic or ideological.

Cultural materialism, theatre and the city

Theatre is symptomatic of its civic culture not simply because of its textual references, however, but also because of its material conditions. Indeed, any given play's textual content and apparent argument are never stable but are profoundly shaped by changing material conditions of production. As Ric Knowles notes in *Reading the Material Theatre* (2004), theatre's meanings 'depend, in part, on the material conditions, both theatrical and cultural, within and through which it is produced and received, conditions which function as its political unconscious, speaking through the performance text whatever its manifest content or intent' (p. 10).

We would expect two very different versions of *Serious Money*, for example, if one was staged during an economic boom in a luxurious theatre crowded with patrons dripping with disposable income and the other during a recession in a poorly resourced theatre before an audience with little money. The former production might affirm protecting the wealth of the rich at the expense of the poor, and the latter might offer an aggressive critique of capitalism. Even the same production witnessed under very different economic conditions would produce different experiences and interpretations. It is therefore necessary to consider theatre productions' material conditions and how they influence the productions' meanings and articulate understandings and experiences of the city.

Cultural materialism

The dominant critical practice used to consider these aspects of theatre and its production of meaning is cultural materialism. Developed from Karl Marx's analysis of systems of production, it has been pursued influentially in cultural studies by Raymond Williams. The first key term, 'culture', emphatically addresses all culture, not just elite 'high culture'. In a 1958 article tellingly entitled 'Culture Is Ordinary', Williams emphasised that 'culture' is all the practices and objects that make up 'a whole way of life', from literature to cinema, television, work and education (p. 76). For our purposes in trying to understand theatre's articulation of urban experience, this approach suggests we should look not just at elite theatre but at theatre and performance in a variety of forms and contexts, as well as at practices of working in and going to the theatre more generally. As Jonathan Dollimore and Alan Sinfield have insisted in their Foreword to *The Shakespeare Myth* (edited by Graham Holderness), cultural materialism's second key term, 'materialism', is 'opposed to "idealism": it insists that culture does not (cannot) transcend the material forces and relations of production' (p. ix). Cultural materialism therefore understands cultural practices – including play texts and theatre events, but also working in theatre, funding it, situating it in the city – 'as inseparable from the conditions of their production and reception in history; and as involved, necessarily, in the making of cultural meanings which are always, finally, political meanings' (p. ix). Cultural materialism can thus help us understand the political and social consequences of our cultural practices, however benign – or, for that matter, malign – they may at first appear.

Cultural materialism in theatre

Cultural materialism has been very influential in theatre analysis. In his 1989 book *Places of Performance*, Marvin Carlson notes, 'The way an audience experiences and interprets a play, we now recognize, is by no means governed solely by what happens on the stage. The entire theatre, its audience arrangements, its other public spaces, its physical appearance, even its location within a city, are all important elements of the process by which an audience makes meaning of its experience' (p. 2). The material conditions of theatre I consider here are space, institutional structures and practices, money and people. These features address where theatre takes place in the city and what that place means; how its architecture signifies; what economies it participates in; and what its demographics are – who works in theatre, in what conditions, and who spends their leisure time there. A cultural materialist analysis concerns itself with material detail to understand not merely what theatre is but, more important, what theatre's political effects are, as well as how they might be changed. This method of analysis indicates how Western urban theatre is complicit with neoliberal capitalism, how it contributes therefore to fostering uneven urban economic and social development, and how its creativity is limited by this complicity.

Places of performance

Where a theatre is located directly affects what it means. This is immediately obvious in New York City, where the received vocabulary for identifying different types of theatre is spatial: there is theatre on the main commercial thoroughfare of Broadway, and there is theatre Off-Broadway, Off-Off-Broadway and so on. This nomenclature poses the overwhelmingly commercial theatre of Broadway/Times Square/42nd Street as the norm against which other sites and the 'other' theatres that happen there are contrasted. Similarly, London has its predominantly commercial West End theatre and its often not-for-profit fringe theatre, and many other major theatre cities likewise distinguish between theatre in central, established commercial areas – the Boulevards of Paris, Toronto's Theatre and Entertainment Districts – and often alternative theatre on the city's margins.

But there is more to these received vocabularies than a simple geographical conveyance of where theatres are located. Theatre's locations, locations' names and the architectural types of theatres predominant in different parts of an urban landscape – all these conditions convey diverse ideological meanings, and they are not necessarily the ideological meanings that the theatres' managements would themselves like to claim. Certainly, some meaning is immediately readable in a theatre's urban location. In Renaissance London, for example, any theatres beyond those at court or the very few licensed to operate within the city's boundaries were only semi-legitimate. They occupied what Carlson calls 'boundary locations – inescapably tied to the city, but never truly a part of it' (p. 70), locations that reflected the theatre's social ambiguity and precariousness in the culture of its time (p. 68). So, whereas theatres that are centrally located and literally incorporated by the city accrue values of social legitimacy, theatres on the margins continue to signify illegitimacy, a signification many fringe theatres cultivate to create associations of outsider identity and radicalism. It is interesting to note in this context that although theatres' locations might remain stable over time, the signification of those locations can shift. London's Globe Theatre is a good example: geographically and socially marginalised by relegation outside the city's limits during the Renaissance, the Globe has now been fully incorporated at the core of London's cultural sphere on the now-fashionable South

Bank, in part as a result of urban expansion and local gentrification, but more importantly because of the ascension of Shakespeare's cultural status.

It is worth interrogating the implicitly assumed attribution of legitimacy and importance – in other words, 'goodness' – to the centrally located theatre that claims it, and the converse attribution of illegitimacy or badness to fringe theatre, because both sets of values are indicative of important ideological forces. Certainly, theatre has increased in legitimacy in the West since the early Renaissance, and this has allowed it to move into a more central position in the urban landscape, reciprocally allowing the city and its ruling authorities to enhance their civic narrative as also being legitimate and good. But in many Western urban contexts we might read the 'good' attributed to the legitimated central urban theatres more accurately as commercial or capitalist, so that it is not only theatre that is endorsed by the idea of goodness attributed to its locations but, problematically, also and simultaneously the commercial priorities of capitalism.

For example, Shaftesbury Avenue, at the core of London's West End, is currently home to six theatres, most of which date from the early twentieth century. But Shaftesbury Avenue's sense of value depends significantly on the authority of London's growing merchant class during the nineteenth century. Previously occupied by slum housing, the area was cleared and the new Shaftesbury Avenue constructed between 1877 and 1896, specifically to create a new thoroughfare for shoppers and merchants travelling from the West End Haymarket northeast to London's expanding bourgeois suburbs. Without city leaders' prioritisation of its merchant classes and their pastimes – commerce, shopping, theatre-going – Shaftesbury Avenue would not exist, though admittedly the key reason the relatively short development took years to complete was because government legislation insisted redevelopment could not begin until slum residents were re-housed ('Shaftesbury Avenue', 1963).

Similarly, Broadway owes its genesis as the site of New York's 'legitimate' theatre to a sense of safety attributable to the commercialism established on this street by the mid-nineteenth century. As Mary C. Henderson observes in her history of New York playhouses, *The City and the Theatre* (2004), by this time, Broadway 'had become the city's prime thoroughfare, paved and lighted', 'served early and well by public transportation', lined with '[i]mposing residences' and – importantly – 'drawing off the principal shops from old city locations into its lower reaches' (p. 77). The emergent Broadway theatre's sense of safety – and therefore propriety and goodness – was in part a function of the street's already established identity as a site of commerce.

By the 1990s, Broadway's theatre provision and identity had grown more diverse. Seeing this as a problem, New York's former mayor Rudolph Giuliani oversaw a notorious development project to clean up 42nd Street and Times Square, billed as an initiative designed to revive and 'improve' the area and its provision of entertainment. But as numerous critics, including David Román, have noted, the project can more forcefully be accused of sanitising the area, driving out the red light district and queer and class-diverse cultures that flourished there to replace them with anaesthetising sites of capitalist consumerism, including a large Toys 'R' Us and the New Amsterdam Theatre. Leased from the city by Disney Theatrical Productions in 1993, the New Amsterdam was extensively refurbished before reopening in 1997, since when it has been home almost continuously to two Disney stage productions, of *The Lion King* and *Mary Poppins* (New York City Theatre.com website).

This complicit relationship between theatre and market ideologies continues in the model of what Carlson calls the 'theatre as public monument' (p. 79), although this model might seem at first to signify that the theatre is on some higher plane, beyond commercial interests. Notable for their 'physical isolation' and 'the multiple vistas' that make them 'landmarks' (p. 79), monumental theatres were established first in France at the end of the eighteenth century but quickly spread as theatre – and France's model of displaying it – gained more widespread cultural approbation. As theatre gains cultural status, city authorities are keener and keener to incorporate and promote it in their city in order to associate that status with their city and their governance. In such contexts, Carlson points out, civic authorities often support the building of monumental theatres 'as highly visible signs of dedication to the arts, especially the arts as defined by the high bourgeois culture of the nineteenth century' (p. 88). Notable examples of monumental theatres are opera houses such as Sydney's, London's enormous brutalist concrete venues at the Royal National

Theatre and the Barbican Centre, Edinburgh's glass-fronted
Festival Theatre and Paris' Théâtre de l'Odéon. The buildings look impressive and monumentally demonstrate a city's
investment in and commitment to the arts and, by extension, its commitment to its citizens' well-being. But might
they actually compromise citizens' well-being?

Some might say yes. Although monumental theatres
might aim to signify civic achievement, that sense of success may certainly not be available to all; indeed, monumental theatres might conversely be seen to dispossess large
numbers of the city's (often poorest) citizens precisely by
displacing them, as did Shaftesbury Avenue's original construction. Carlson shows, for example, that because theatres can signify the types of cultural values civic authorities
often want to nurture – signs of success, affluence, elitism –
urban planners often develop theatres and other cultural
complexes to gentrify poorer urban districts, but in so
doing they may make little provision for what and whom the
development displaces. New York's Lincoln Center for the
Performing Arts, for instance, was built during the 1960s
in part to regenerate and gentrify mid-town Manhattan,
but its development entailed demolishing low-rent housing (pp. 92–4). London's Barbican Centre, similarly, was
built on an area devastated by Second World War bombing.
But instead of replacing the low-cost housing that had been
there before, the Barbican's redevelopment, opened in 1982,
brought in tower blocks of expensive private apartments
and an arts complex where programming is arguably aimed
less at comparatively poor immigrants still neighbouring

the Barbican to the north and east and more at those on
its southern flank: comparatively wealthy City workers –
Small Metal Objects' executives and *Serious Money*'s traders. The issue is not just that monumental theatres literally
displace already dispossessed urban citizens – though that's
bad enough. What these theatres reinforce is a set of ideological priorities that again legitimate so-called free market
economics and priorities, even where those might not be
best for all. In a deregulated housing market, what's to stop
speculators investing in an arts complex that will attract
buyers to comparatively expensive apartments in the same
complex? Why should the displaced former tenants be the
developers' concern?

Thus, although many central, urban and even commercial theatres may appear to be left-leaning – theatres
such as the Royal Court in London, which first produced
Churchill's *Serious Money*, but also London's Royal National,
Glasgow's Citizens, Toronto's Tarragon and Edinburgh's
Traverse – the ostensible project of a play or even a theatre
company can be undermined or radically altered by how
that play or theatre actually works in its urban surround-
ings, in its material context of production. The design and
location of a theatre can ascribe an ideological endorsement
of market economics to that theatre, even when the shows
it produces might seem to argue for a different politics, for
example one that is apparently benign (promoting affluence)
or even anti-capitalist, as we might read *Serious Money* and
Small Metal Objects. *Small Metal Objects*' de-centred location, after all, was only temporary, scarcely shaking the

formidable City-based foundations of the Barbican Centre. A cultural materialist reading of theatre in its geo-social context thus reveals that the attribution of 'goodness' to central urban theatre – such as that on Broadway or in London's West End – risks conflating positive value with neoliberal market priorities and their threat of vicious economic and social inequality.

Theatre capital

We can see a similar pattern in contemporary Western cities' theatre economies, which tend to reproduce an aesthetically conservative theatre culture that reinforces consumer capitalism.

Theatre's economies have to do with how it pays its production costs, including the costs of buying or renting and maintaining rehearsal and production space, building and maintaining sets and costume, purchasing and renting equipment, and paying staff salaries and fees. As Tracy C. Davis observes in *The Economics of the British Stage, 1800–1914* (2000), without money, 'there would be no dramatists, no actors, no payroll, no real estate, nothing. ... No pay, no play' (pp. 18–19). To raise production capital, theatre in the contemporary West relies on a combination of state subsidy, private sponsorship and box office revenue. The non-subsidised commercial theatre sector most clearly operates according to recognisable free market economics. Although the free market hypothetically stimulates the production of the best – because most competitive – products, it can tend to produce what investors believe will be the most reliably saleable products. The fact they are saleable might mean they are good, but it might also mean they are merely familiar or fashionable or have a star cast member. The free market's reliance on saleability is acutely felt in the theatre because theatre relies on substantial initial speculative investment in show development, long before producers can expect to realise any profit through ticket sales.

The result of this so-called free market economy is a theatre culture which, in aiming to be popular, tends to become overwhelmingly populist. Innovation is generally devalued and familiar 'classics' are repeatedly re-staged, producing what Susan Bennett, in *Theatre Audiences* (1997), calls 'repertory standardisation' (see pp. 108–12). In *Theatre Ecology* (2007), Baz Kershaw explores how British theatre within the neoliberal economy of *Serious Money*'s 1980s saw an increase in the production of populist fare such as musicals, revivals of previously successful plays and adaptations of well-known novels (p. 167). In such contexts, successful shows often see their runs extended, sometimes for years, as in the examples of *Cats* (1981, New London Theatre, London), which played in London for twenty-one years and New York for eighteen, and *Les Misérables*, which celebrated its twenty-third anniversary in London in 2008. The extended run can doubly reinforce theatrical conservatism by daily repeating the same show and thereby preventing the theatre in which it is produced (*ad nauseam*) from being available to produce another, different, perhaps culturally more up-to-date show. Transfers often move from the not-for-profit sector (where they were developed with state funding – or citizens' tax subsidy) to what we might call the now-for-profit commercial sector. Once here, profits can go to entrepreneur producers whose only financial risk has been to organise the transfer of an already proven product.

As the free market economy continues to go global, the market of the theatre economy has gone global as well, again with often conservative, homogenising effects. The global megamusical economy has produced franchising, which sees individual megamusicals reproduced as near as possibly identically in cities around the world, flooding the global theatre market with the same product. As Andrew Lloyd Webber's Really Useful Group website proudly proclaims, 'Since its opening in London in 1981, Cats has been presented in over twenty countries and in about two hundred and fifty cities, including such diverse destinations as Buenos Aires, Seoul, Helsinki and Singapore'; 'most productions replicate the original show as closely as possible' (www.reallyuseful.com). Where megamusical production is not franchised in replica copies it is instead often toured, usually at enormous expense, reinforcing the need for market success. Sheridan Morley notes in Theatre's Strangest Acts (2006) that when The Phantom of the Opera 'moves to a new theatre, the touring production needs 27 articulated lorries to transfer the set' (p. 164). The resulting cost is both financial and ecological, as Kershaw observes in Theatre Ecology (p. 157). This is not to say that good shows should not tour; in fact, we might argue that because touring them can be beneficial to the new audiences who get to see them, touring is a kind of recycling that is precisely ecological.

But what I do mean to question in this economy is what the criteria are for deciding that a show is 'good' and deserves to tour, and how this kind of recycling inhibits innovation, diversity, genuine consumer choice and *distinctive* productions that are specifically relevant to different cities and audiences around the world. (For more on megamusicals, see Dan Rebellato's *Theatre & Globalization*, 2009.)

The megamusical's principle of touring in search of new markets is practised increasingly by other – perhaps not so obviously conservative – theatre as well, but again with neutralising cultural effects. Indeed, some of the world's best-known theatrical innovators increasingly rely on raising production capital through co-production agreements with a range of international venues and a commitment to tour internationally, often to a succession of city festivals. In this case, despite the theatre maker's reputation as an innovator, the requirements of touring may discourage innovations in production from the outset, as the show needs to remain comprehensible in a range of global contexts. In *Reading the Material Theatre*, Knowles notes that touring to international festivals performances which resonated with cultural specificity in their original sites of production can have the effect of generalising those performances' meanings as simply resonant of their origins' 'local colour' or, even more broadly, as representative of national identity (p. 182). In other words, the shows are simplified, extending a simplification/commoditisation only too familiar in the logos – *Phantom*'s half-mask, *Les Mis*' waif, *Cats*' face – that proliferate through marketing strategies for musicals in particular (Kershaw,

Theatre Ecology, p. 169). William Talen (also known as Reverend Billy, whom I discuss in more detail below) has forlornly observed, 'Now the lights of Broadway shine for shows that are nothing but long commercial breaks. They are movies adapted to the stage, mostly. These are merchandising vehicles' (*What Should I Do ...*, 2003, pp. 31–2).

If the commercial sector's competitiveness is apparently so ruthlessly homogenising, generalising and conservative, we might turn hopefully to the state-subsidised sector in search of innovation and diversity for urban theatre artists and audiences. Unfortunately, here too we find a competitive market with many of the same problems as the commercial sector. Subsidised theatre competes in a mixed market with commercial work, and subsidy only ever covers a part of its costs; the UK's Royal Shakespeare Company, for example, meets only half its costs through subsidy (*Annual Report and Accounts, 2007/08*, p. 34). Even within the subsidised theatre sector there is competition for state funding. And anxiety about risk combined with the desire to leave a tangible, ideally monumental legacy can mean state investors are sometimes more willing to invest in theatre buildings than productions. From the mid-1990s into the twenty-first century, this attitude was manifested in the UK in the government's investment of funds raised though the National Lottery in capital projects (such as building construction or renovation) rather than production. One result was that magnificent, monumental, new theatres sometimes struggled to support production.

Theatre people: audiences

At the same time that current Western urban theatre economies overwhelmingly encourage (or produce) conservative populism, they reinforce the class stratification that has long been materially embedded in theatre buildings, as in civic spaces and neighbourhoods. For example, the theatres of the eighteenth and nineteenth centuries had (and often retain) not only different bars for audience groups paying different ticket prices but different entrances as well, with glamorous entrances for elite, high-paying patrons and dingy stairwells entered off alleyways for servant-class punters with cheap tickets.

Even where such snobberies of built-in class stratification have been physically excised from a twentieth-century theatre architecture keen to be – or certainly to appear – more democratic, class stratification continues through variable ticket pricing. As Deborah Cook observes in *The Culture Industry Revisited* (1996), 'Commodified culture offers the economically disempowered middle class the narcissistic illusion that it still has power and prestige' (p. 13). Audiences are still spatially segregated according to how much they have paid, with higher-priced tickets generally purchasing seats with better and more comfortable views of the performance space. In the nineteenth-century theatre, the pit went through its own form of slum clearance gentrification. Formerly occupied by working-class audiences, who were moved to the top of the theatres (just as they often lived in attic rooms in their employers' townhouses), the pit became the stalls, complete with plush seating for bourgeois comfort. This transformation also took the elite classes out of their boxes – modelled on private domestic spaces – and put them on display in a new kind of civic arena. Variable ticket pricing not only separates audiences within theatres but can also, of course, exclude audiences who cannot pay. Theatre can convey to its audiences a sense of cultural capital – of cultural knowledge, understanding, entitlement and mobility. And in an expensive theatre economy like the one that has proliferated in the Western city in the age of the global megamusical, some people simply do not have access to that capital. We are variably enfranchised and disenfranchised according to whether we can pay.

Theatre people: workers

People who are not from big cities often move there for work opportunities, not least the chance to act in the theatre. William Talen/Reverend Billy is hardly alone in claiming, 'I had moved across the country with all the expectations that can be assigned to New York City.' He came to Broadway because he 'thought it was the center of any actor's world' (*What Should I Do ...*, p. 30). But what, really, does it mean to work in the theatre? Does the labour economy of contemporary urban theatre also reinforce capitalism and its attendant class stratifications, which advantage some while disadvantaging others? In many ways, yes.

Like the ways theatre has historically treated its audiences, its treatment of workers has in many respects improved, especially in the past century or so. Throughout the history of Western theatre, there have always been some celebrated actors, but for the most part, working in the theatre, especially as a performer, has been considered disreputable or worse. Even in late-Victorian England, when some actors achieved significant respectability, the extension of such privilege across the acting profession was quite limited. In *Actresses as Working Women* (1991), Tracy C. Davis notes, 'The reality for most [actors, especially women] was a low working-class wage, social ostracism, and the constant threat of unemployment' (p. xiii). Gradually, actors' professional security and welfare have improved with the integration of systems of 'unemployment insurance, sickness benefits, disability pensions, and superannuation' (p. xiv), initially through charities and later through unions.

Nevertheless, the theatre in the urban West still operates a labour economy which is uneven: it is disadvantageous for the vast majority of actors outside the small number who attract celebrity salaries and constant employment. This is so because the economy remains organised around competition, epitomised in the audition process. To remain available to compete whenever a suitable audition comes up, so-called resting actors between acting contracts generally do anything but rest, needing to take jobs, but jobs that are flexible so they can be dropped at short notice. The actor's typical 'resting' jobs – office temp, cleaner, waiter – are indeed comparatively flexible, but also therefore comparatively insecure and ill-paid.

The actor's labour is devalued in other ways as well. In *Stage Fright, Animals, and Other Theatrical Problems* (2006), Nicholas Ridout explores 'problems' of the modern theatre, arguing in part that they evidence theatre makers' and audiences' exploration of feelings about work. For Ridout, the actor's conditions of work are replete with problems. The actor's time is rigorously constrained by schedules (pre-show and interval calls, cues and so on); the labour of line-learning, rehearsal and performance is profoundly repetitive; wage level differentiation sustains gross differences between celebrities and minimum-wage-earning bit players, and this differentiation is unchallengeable because of the acting market's 'huge pool of surplus labour'; and 'the core activity itself is both a metaphor of alienation and alienation itself: the actor is paid to appear in public speaking words written by someone else and executing physical movement which has at the very least usually been subject to intense and critical scrutiny by a representative of the management who effectively enjoys the power of hiring and firing'. Ridout concludes, 'The actor is both sign and referent of the wholly alienated wage slave' (p. 100). Talen's dream of self-fulfilment through becoming an actor in the big city may be widely shared, but, for Ridout, the reality of such work in a competitive capitalist economy is profoundly alienating and, in some ways, self-defeating.

Cultural materialist practice evaluated

There are a number of advantages to cultural materialist analysis when we consider how theatre functions in the city socially, economically and ideologically. Most important, it helps identify how theatre's meanings are radically constrained by material conditions of production. Drama's textual meaning can never be conveyed directly or solely through production; other meanings accrue in production. Nor is the apparent mission of any given theatre necessarily the meaning it will consistently achieve in production. These points matter because although much theatre might appear to be socially aware and socially concerned – the good usually triumph, after all, as in *Les Mis* and, in some ways, *Small Metal Objects* – its *practices*, and therefore its meanings, may not all be equally socially aware and concerned.

I have argued that the material conditions that overwhelmingly pertain in the predominantly service-based economies of the cities of the West consistently reproduce late-capitalist neoliberal ideologies. They reinforce class stratification through pricing, wage differentiation, architectural design and processes of gentrification which displace poorer communities. They stimulate the reproduction of assembly-line-like commodity theatre, a trend recognisable most obviously in globalised replica musicals, but evident too in many more parts of the theatre industry, where high costs in competitive economies quell creativity by requiring the mass production of more, new – but familiar and populist – products. They impose further uniformity on production by demanding shows be accessible to globalised audiences of tourists and international festival audiences. They stimulate consumerism by contributing to the development of thoroughfares and neighbourhoods devoted to tourism, leisure and entertainment, and by producing spin-off commodities, such as T-shirts and programmes, which extend a process of simplifying/commoditising already begun by the replica shows themselves. They tie workers into disadvantageous conditions because actors know only too well they are competing in a market saturated with surplus labour/resting actors.

As much of my vocabulary in the preceding pages and paragraph should make clear, in many, many respects I do not believe that the reification of neoliberal capitalism through theatre in the city is fundamentally a good thing. The competition championed by capitalism's supporters produces not choice but merely a sense of choice in a market that may indeed be swollen, but with uniformity. The 'good' resulting from conditions of 'free' competition is ideologically overwritten with 'bad' class differentiations. Opportunity is limited not infinite. Using cultural materialist analytic strategies, we can diagnose the functioning of urban cultural practice beyond what it is 'obviously' doing – making 'good' theatre; we can diagnose the functioning of dominant urban ideologies to see what their material, ideological and cultural impacts are; and we can see how the meanings of theatre practice are intricately embedded in urban ideologies. As much as theatre – in the subsidised sector especially – might claim to stand in active opposition to dominant market ideologies, my cultural materialist analysis suggests there is no such outside to occupy. I have concentrated here on the ways that cultural materialism can be used to explore how theatre in Western post-industrial cities reproduces one set of ideologies that are capitalist. I have done this to maintain focus in such a short book, but more importantly because I think it matters that our urban cultural practices such as theatre – apparently so benign and, because it is subsidised, operating at least in part beyond the whim of market forces – not only reproduce but naturalise capitalist ideologies and their pernicious, divisive social effects. This said, it is worth noting that cultural materialism certainly can be – and has been – deployed to explore how theatre produces other aspects of social power dynamics relating to, for example, gender, race, ethnicity, dis/ability and age.

Despite the many values of cultural materialism, as a critical approach it has limits. In the previous paragraph, for example, I suggest that it is impossible to stand in opposition to and outside of dominant market ideologies because 'there is no such outside to occupy'. But that is a rather defeatist position, and not cultural materialism's full story in any case. One problem with the foregoing analysis and its method, therefore, is that it can be almost totalising in its negativity or, even, cynicism. It can paint a picture of the role of theatre in the city where citizens and audiences seem to be inevitably caught in an oppressive, exploitative, uncreative culture with no opportunity to escape its hold, challenge its exploitations or be creative. It can assume that because capitalist conditions are widespread, they are totalising and cannot be disrupted, even from within. It focuses on commercial (and some subsidised) theatre but not the full range of theatre and performance, some of which might more effectively challenge hegemonic practices and ideologies. It focuses on material conditions, perhaps to the exclusion of other relevant conditions such as how theatre makes us feel and behave.

Perhaps most significant, it does not account for how we might more properly identify capitalism as not total but volatile, unstable and incomplete. As Michael McKinnie notes in *City Stages* (2007), marketisation 'is never entirely successful'. Because it requires subjects' 'submission as labour to capitalist-determined wages, time, and space', people within this economy are actually 'frequently disobedient' (p. 10) – consider the rise of the 'duvet day' and the long-established long lunch. As Karl Marx and Friedrich Engels famously predicted in the mid-nineteenth century in *The Communist Manifesto*, the fundamental contradictions of capitalism – especially its gross exploitation of an oppressed labouring class – inevitably produce class conflict that ultimately destroys capitalism itself. The *Manifesto* concludes: 'The proletariat have nothing to lose but their chains. They have a world to win. WORKING MEN OF ALL COUNTRIES, UNITE!' (p. 77).

Admittedly, capitalism has not yet been destroyed, but it is rife with instability, not least as witnessed in the global economic crash of autumn 2008. So we might usefully rethink our cultural materialist analysis – particularly how we understand material conditions functioning to constrain – as less totalising. What else can be accommodated if we do this? We might start by looking for theatre and performance that do some of the things I suggested two paragraphs above – that is, theatre and performance that might, first, more effectively challenge hegemonic practices and ideologies and be more liberating and, second, help us focus on how theatre makes us feel and behave. Further, we might explore an alternative critical practice which focuses on such performance and how it makes us feel: performative analysis.

City and performativity: performing the city

In contrast to cultural materialist analysis, performative analysis concentrates overwhelmingly on the ways people can and do act with freedom to self-author, exercising agency, control and power through everyday acts of self-articulation and self-creation. It does not generally see subjects as materially and socially trapped in restrictive, oppressive, self-denying social contexts already determined by the oppressions of inescapable material circumstances; it sees opportunities to challenge those conditions.

The term 'performative' was developed in linguistic studies in recognition that language does not merely describe things; in many ways, it actually makes them exist. Linguist J. L. Austin argued that 'speech acts' have some perlocutionary force, or *do* things. In *How to Do Things with Words* (1975), Austin called this force 'performativity': 'the issuing of the utterance is the performing of an action' (p. 6). Speech acts include bets, promises and oaths, all of which do not merely describe the world but change it, by committing the speaker to his or her claim and establishing a more or less formal relationship between the speaker and someone else. Examples of speech acts offered by Austin in *How to Do Things with Words* include 'I bet' and 'I declare war' (p. 7); in saying the phrase, the speaker enacts it. Language is performative because its speaking produces what it claims.

This idea that the doing (or performance) of something produces an effect has been crucial to theories of performativity beyond linguistics, because it establishes that other acts too can have force. For example, a salute is a gesture which establishes social relationships, not least the subordination of the one who salutes to the one saluted. Everyday gestures such as how we walk or dress may at first seem to have less force because they are apparently so normal. Many critics have argued, however, that such behaviours have more force because they are not normal but normalising, actively establishing certain behaviours as normal and others as strange, though neither is essentially given.

The concept of performativity has had enormous impact in gender and feminist studies in particular, where it has been taken up most influentially by philosopher Judith Butler. In *Gender Trouble* (1999), Butler argues that although gender identities may often feel socially and biologically fixed – so trapping women and men in limiting stereotypes and behaviours – we are actually constantly performing such identities, actively creating them. We tend to reproduce received and oppressive stereotypes because we have been socially conditioned to do so through the disciplining forces of schooling, family life, etiquette, law, fashion, advertising imagery and so on. But we also have some opportunity to conceive and perform other forms of these identities too, and thus to recreate gender identities in formations that are less socially restrictive. Butler argued that gender is not given but socially constructed; it is 'a *stylized repetition of acts*' that we reproduce daily in conventional everyday behaviour

(p. 179, italics original). It is therefore possible that, within limits, we are all, in our various ways, drag artists, making up ways of performing our genders. Normative behaviour is extremely powerful, so we may not transform it overnight, but we can trouble hegemonic understandings and practices of gender, challenging their legitimacy.

Urban studies

This core idea that we can act with liberty and agency to alter the ways we act in everyday life, thereby to a degree at least controlling who we are, was pioneered in urban studies, in terms of understanding how cities' identities are socially produced through the ways we act in them and also how individuals' identities are produced in the city. Some of this analysis considers how hegemonic institutions such as state and crown use public urban performance to reinforce their authority. There is an extensive literature, for example, on the Renaissance practice of staging a monarch's royal entry into a city with enormous and expensive fanfare, including decorations, music, feasts, carriages and performances, all designed quite visibly to impress, thereby creating royal authority by performing it. (See, for example, Carlson, *Places of Performance*, pp. 19ff; Kipling, 'Wonderfull Spectacles', 1997.) As David Welch proposes in *Propaganda and the German Cinema 1933–1945* (1983), we might think similarly of the infamous Nuremberg Party rallies which extended Hitler's cult of the Führer through both live events and the distribution of Leni Riefenstahl's propagandist documentary film *Triumph of the Will* (1935). We might also think of ceremonies for inaugurating presidents, opening parliaments and launching new shopping malls or 'flagship' stores. Such events coercively legitimate the object they honour precisely by celebrating it publicly in a ritual that virtually demands audience cooperation and consensus. Achieving similar effects but in much less spectacular (and therefore possibly subtler) ways are everyday events which naturalise what they celebrate. Here we might consider, for example, the frenzied trading that takes place daily in stock exchanges worldwide, is depicted in all its brash exuberance in *Serious Money* and legitimates the Northern hemisphere's gambling with the South's debt or, for that matter, wealthy Westerners gambling with poorer Westerners' debts. As I do in the final chapter of my book *Staging the UK* (2005), we might re-examine the ways cities are often riddled with statues of former leaders who are by now regarded with indifference at best and sometimes contempt. And we might re-evaluate the ways the architecture of cities' central financial districts constantly declares its authority through a physical presence that is silent and solemn — but monumental and foreboding.

Before this section of *Theatre & the City* begins to sound as pessimistic about the urban intractability of ruling-class ideology as the previous section on cultural materialism, I hasten to note that theories of performativity in urban studies have overwhelmingly been deployed to explore its utopian potentials for challenging hegemonic oppression. A key character in this counter-discourse is the *flâneur*, who confounds dominant uses of the city by casually strolling through it, making his own pathways through it, and so his own *version* of it through his manner of performing it. (The *flâneur* is notoriously male.) Nineteenth-century writer Charles Baudelaire coined the term – which literally means 'stroller' or 'idler' – to describe the ambling challenge made by some of his peers and himself to the order they felt was increasingly being imposed on Paris by both the state and the market. German critic Walter Benjamin took up the term in the 1930s in his writing on Baudelaire and in his own enormous *Arcades Project*, which documented the ways an increasingly powerful consumer culture was damaging the city by limiting its cultural variety and utopian potential.

A variation on this kind of walking is the *dérive* – or 'drifting' – which follows the walker's desire paths in a process variously called 'psychic landscaping' or 'psycho-geography' – all terms that emphasise the walker's pleasure and agency. In 1950s Paris, artist-intellectual inheritors of surrealism advocated the *dérive* as a way to transform 'everyday life from a realm of bland consumption to free creation', as Sadie Plant puts it in *The Most Radical Gesture* (1992, p. 5). Grouped collectively from 1957 as the Situationist International, these activists saw society as dominated not just by commodity production but by consumption, of goods as well as spectacle. In his influential book, *The Society of the Spectacle* (1994), the Situationist International's self-styled leader, Guy Debord, emphasised, 'The spectacle is not a collection of images; rather, it is a social relationship between people that is mediated by images' (Thesis 4, p. 12). As Plant puts it, the situationists

> argued that the alienation fundamental to class society and capitalist production has permeated all areas of social life, knowledge, and culture, with the consequence that people are removed and alienated not only from the goods they produce and consume, but also from their own experiences, emotions, creativity, and desires. People are spectators of their own lives, and even the most personal gestures are experienced at one remove. (p. 1)

For Debord, society was subjected to multiple cumulative degradations; where once it might have been about being, it was then about consuming, and then about appearing (Thesis 17, p. 16). The situationists' interventions aimed at transforming capitalist society were, therefore, acts meant to be seen and to see things differently. The *Situationist International Anthology* (2006), edited by Ken Knabb, documents examples such as graffiti denouncing work by reminding pedestrians, 'Under the paving stones, the beach!', and exhorting, 'Workers of all countries, enjoy!' (pp. 448–9), and excerpts from the situationists' journal, which was full of advertising playfully ridiculing advertising. The situationists' interventions were strongly visible in the protests in Paris in May 1968.

Around the world in this same year there was a widespread sense of increased state oppression and corruption: in the USA, opposition to the war in Vietnam mounted, as did racial tension and rioting; in England, politician Enoch Powell made his racist 'Rivers of Blood' speech; Czechoslovakia's 'Prague Spring' of reform was quashed by a Soviet invasion and the reassertion of a more oppressive regime; and in France, there were major strikes. There were numerous and widespread social protests, such as those of the Black Power movement in the USA and the student protests in France. In this context in France, the idea of the city as a place where social practices could transform social relationships in and with the city, wrangling control of the city back into the hands of the people from state powers — and particularly from capitalist ideologies — gained particular purchase.

Writing in France before and after the (ultimately suppressed) Paris riots, Debord's one-time mentor Henri Lefebvre observed that urban society was increasingly being organised in ways that oppressed its occupants. It constrained them as labourers within a capitalist economy and spatially shunted them between functional places dedicated to labour and isolating dormitory communities dedicated to bodily recuperation for more labour tomorrow. As political geographer Edward Soja observes in *Postmodern Geographies* (1989), 'The very survival of capitalism, Lefebvre argued, was built upon the creation of an increasingly embracing, instrumental, and socially mystified spatiality, hidden from critical view under thick veils of illusion and ideology' (p. 50).

But the oppression of this ordered condition, Lefebvre proposed, was not total or consistent. Like the situationists, he believed the city's streets offered opportunities for genuine social interaction, resistance and disorder, for play rather than work and for (social) use rather than (economic) exchange. In the streets, people could reclaim a renewed urban society and their 'right to the city' (the title of one of his books published in 1968, selections from which appear in translation in his *Writings on Cities*, 1996). 'What about the street?' he asked rhetorically in 1970's *The Urban Revolution*.

> It serves as a meeting place (topos), for without it no other designated encounters are possible (cafés, theaters, halls). These places animate the street and are served by its animation, or they cease to exist. In the street, a form of spontaneous theater, I become spectacle and spectator, and sometimes an actor. The street is where movement takes place, the interaction without which urban life would not exist, leaving only separation, a forced and fixed segregation. And there are consequences to eliminating the street...: the extinction of life, the reduction of the city to a dormitory, the aberrant functionalization of existence. ...The street is a place to play and learn. The street is disorder. ...This disorder is alive. It informs. It surprises. ...Revolutionary events generally take place in the street. (pp. 18–19)

Nevertheless, he recognised that the street was also compromised by its gradual integration into a culture of consumption:

> The street became a network organized for and by consumption. The rate of pedestrian circulation, although still tolerated, was determined and measured by the ability to perceive store windows and buy the objects displayed in them. Time became 'merchandise time' (time for buying and selling, time bought and sold). The street regulated time outside of work; it subjected it to the same system, the system of yield and profit. It was nothing more than the necessary transition between forced labor, programmed leisure, and habitation as a place of consumption. (p. 20)

As commentators Michael Keith and Steve Pile argue in *Place and the Politics of Identity* (1993), Lefebvre recognised the city 'as both crucible of conflict and container of dissent' (p. 25). That said, conflict and dissent were possible there and to be practised through people's daily urban resistance to state- and market-modelled ways of being. Instead of submission to capitalist labour's segregation of individuals and its invitation to see ourselves as isolated individual and/or family units, Lefebvre advocated an understanding of society as a civic community with collective power. He also advocated play and creativity in the face of work.

What continues to resonate from the work of these twentieth-century continental European theorists is an analysis which claims that the social oppressions of capitalism (and then Debord's capitalist society of spectacle) are reproduced through the configurations of urban society, that urban society therefore has to change, but that such change is precisely possible through the socially resistant, challenging practices of urban performativity.

Happenings

The example of these European activists who wanted to change social life in the city through performative interventions had wide impact. In 1960s America, their example resonated in performances, often staged in public, called 'happenings'. Happenings eschewed theatrical and fine art conventions, avoided linear plotting and realistic characterisation, could appear illogical and collage-like, and usually involved a handful of performers, as themselves, executing a variety of tasks derived from the everyday and not intended to appear fictional. For example, as one of their early advocates and documenters Michael Kirby suggests, the performer 'walks with boxes on his feet, rides a bicycle, empties a suspended bucket of milk on his head' (*Happenings*, 1965, p. 17). Happenings disrupted the conventions – and conventionalism – of both theatrical performance and gallery-based art practices that were then standard. One of the founding artists, Allan Kaprow, argues in *Essays on the Blurring of Art and Life* (2003) that happenings eschewed conventional audience/performer separation, were grounded in chance not set texts, and delighted in their ephemerality, refusing the commoditisation of art in the market space of the gallery (pp. 15–26). And like the interventions of the situationists, happenings were somewhat surreal, they occupied the streets in part to reclaim them, and they validated everyday actions as constitutive of life and its meanings by 'blurring art and life', wilfully and mischievously performing everyday actions themselves. Happenings embraced the idea that everyday performance is performative, constituting us in and through our behaviour, and they demonstrated that by performing in extraordinary ways it is possible to disrupt the naturalised meanings and behaviours of public space and 'ordinary' social life.

Performativity in the city now

The explicitly alternative culture in which the Situationist International and happenings flourished dissipated over the ensuing decades. But there remains an abundance of performance work which shares many of the formal characteristics and performative ambitions of the work of these movements while extending their practices in the context of changed circumstances and new challenges. Very important among these new circumstances is the extension of communications technologies. These create more forums for more widespread commodity advertising and exchange (think eBay). And they allow us to communicate more through mediation than through face-to-face encounter in a process Raymond Williams presciently called 'mobile privatisation' in his 1974 book *Television* (p. 19) (think Facebook and other social networking sites). In other words, they potentially intensify the social alienation envisaged in Debord's *Society of the Spectacle*. At the same time, they also create more contexts for performative intervention, for coordinating communication in the planning of resistant performative practices and for new digital psycho-geographies, where we can follow hyperlink desire paths of our choice as cyber-*flâneurs*. What's the balance of these effects, and how do they affect social life in the contemporary city? I explore these questions through an examination of three forms of contemporary performative practice that inherit features from the preceding practices outlined above and that demonstrate the continuing – even flourishing – vigour of performative political interventions in contemporary urban performance. These three forms are the performance walk, protest and what we might call – in relation to Augusto Boal's invisible theatre, with which it shares political aims but in contrast to which it ostentatiously draws attention to itself – the high-visibility performative intervention.

The *dérive* now: the performance walk

One type of politicised performance practice that has proliferated recently is the performance walk. This takes at least two forms: in one, an artist or company follows an itinerary through the city and somehow presents that to an audience, often just the audience of passers-by who happen to see the walk itself or its subsequent documentation. Belgium-born, Mexico-based artist Francis Alÿs makes numerous pieces which, in direct homage to his *flâneur* predecessors, he calls in Spanish *paseos* ('strolls'); many are documented in his monograph *Francis Alÿs: Seven Walks: London, 2004–5* (2005). In 1996, he carried a leaking paint can through São Paulo (*The Leak*); in 1997, he pushed an ice block through Mexico City, until it and its trace gradually melted away (*Paradox of Praxis*); in 1998, he trailed an unwinding knitted jumper through Stockholm (*the winner/the loser*); in 2005, he trooped an English regiment on an unplanned route through the City of London (*Guards*, part of *Seven Walks*). He literally marked his path through each city, making temporarily visible and literally remarkable the kind of journey people make every day, especially as pedestrians.

The second type of performance walk conscripts one or more audience members at a time to follow an urban itinerary scripted by an artist or company. We can see precedents for this form in Medieval drama – where audiences would walk around a series of pageants to follow a developing story – and in the promenade theatre that has carried on down from it through the twentieth century to now. We can also see precedents in the *flâneur* and the *dérive*, both of which conceived walking in the city as a way to create it anew by rejecting the types of priorities a city dominated by capital and spectacle might try to impose. Other key influences include British theatre artist Fiona Templeton's famous *YOU – The City* (1990), which her website calls 'an intimate citywide play for an audience of one'. Performed first in Manhattan in 1988, it has subsequently been performed in London and around Europe. In *YOU – The City*, one audience member at a time follows a scripted route of encounters through a series of public and private urban spaces. In Manhattan, the 'client' (audience member) started the show in an office on midtown Times Square and moved through various encounters in locations that included a church, a taxi ride to downtown Hell's Kitchen, a playground and an apartment. The piece invited the client to be explicitly self-reflexive about everyday urban encounters and journeys she or he would probably usually make without particular notice. And by casting the client as a performer, the piece invited 'YOU' to consider your relationship to the city as not passive but active, performative in the sense that YOU could see how your responses to the people and environments encountered might affect the show, yourself and the city.

It is this casting of the audience member as the central performer in *YOU – The City* that has been most vigorously taken up in more recent performance work. In part because of developments in technology, though, a key feature of this proliferating form is that the theatre maker can be absent; the maker or company provides a script, most commonly as an audio recording, that the audience member enacts, alone, among passing pedestrians. The audience member becomes a solo performer and is deliberately isolated in the city, inviting reflection on the ways that the city and communications technologies produce isolation and possible social atomisation or civic encounter and communication.

Rider Spoke

A recent example of this kind of performance (on bikes rather than on foot) is Blast Theory's *Rider Spoke*. Blast

Theory is an increasingly well-known British company dedicated to exploring the use of interactive media in performance, particularly in the inner city (www.blastheory.co.uk). In *Uncle Roy All Around You* (Institute of Contemporary Arts, London, 2003), individual audience members were given handheld gaming consoles with which they tried to track down Uncle Roy in the centre of a city and simultaneously were themselves tracked by remote audiences online through the use of GPS. *Rider Spoke* was hosted by the Barbican in autumn 2007. Audience members reported to the Barbican lobby to borrow a bicycle (if we hadn't brought one) with a mini-computer with speakers and microphone mounted on the handlebars. We then cycled into the surrounding city in whatever direction we individually chose. Instructions arrived via the computer, mostly inviting us to respond to questions verbally over the mic or to find places where previous cyclist-audience members had recorded answers and hear those played back. Instructions were personal: tell your name and what you look like; say how revealing a secret would affect you. And they were about personal responses to the built environment: find a building you like, describe it and say what you will do there; find a place that smells and describe it. Of course, it was not necessary to tell the truth, and answers I heard were poetic, funny and inventive. On a clear, mild evening, I enjoyed cycling around the city listening to and making up stories.

Like the *flâneur*, *Rider Spoke*'s cyclist re-maps the city according to his or her own feelings, desires, curiosities and stories. This personalised map can deviate from hegemonic mappings – of streets prioritised for motorised traffic – and from linear mappings – of routes designed to provide efficient travel between work and home, to seduce us into consumer behaviour or to show the city and its economic priorities off to best (most seductive) advantage. In Debord's 'society of the spectacle', *Rider Spoke* invited us not only to look at the city but also to listen to its stories. It traded conventional City priorities – commerce, work, clear and functional routes to set destinations, the visual over the aural – for unconventional priorities – feelings, leisure, wandering, sound and a bicycle-based perspective over one dominated by motorised vehicles. It also appropriated technology from its potential to separate us socially, using it instead to facilitate a sense of community, intimacy and shared freedom in the city.

Protest now

Blast Theory's championing of both bicycle and cyclist is, of course, part of a much larger current movement that advocates cycling, which is itself part of an even larger movement against the car's depletion of the world's natural resources, its contribution to climate change and its participation in global free trade which exploits impoverished labour markets. These movements have consistently used performative mass protests to publicise their causes and, they hope, to change attitudes, behaviours and the future. They are thus part of a long history of public protest and also of the enormous, loose category of street performance. As Jan Cohen-Cruz's anthology *Radical Street Performance* (1998) makes clear, street performance can take myriad forms, from puppet shows to demonstrations, rallies, parades, pageants, circuses, and guerrilla and invisible theatre. And as her adjective 'radical' indicates, these forms often 'question or re-envision ingrained social arrangements of power' (p. 1). In *The Radical in Performance* (1999), Baz Kershaw suggests that public protest increasingly incorporates performance practices to achieve performative (transforming) effects. Furthermore, he argues that although it may be true that from the beginning of the 1990s there has been less overtly political – or agit prop – theatre than there was in the 1970s and 1980s, it is also true that more overt political action such as protesting has since become increasingly theatricalised or performative, demonstrating the ongoing (if shifted) importance of theatre and performance to political change.

Critical Mass

Critical Mass started in the early 1990s as a movement of mass bike rides that take place on the same day each month in cities around the world, often with hundreds of riders in any given city (see www.critical-mass.org; Carlsson, ed., *Critical Mass*, 2002). In a sense, Lefebvre predicted the advent of Critical Mass when he wrote in *The Urban Revolution*,

> The street is more than just a place for movement and circulation. The invasion of the automobile and the pressure of the automobile lobby have turned the car into a key object, parking into an obsession, traffic into a priority, harmful to urban

and social life. The day is approaching when we
will be forced to limit the rights and powers of
the automobile. Naturally, this won't be easy, and
the fallout will be considerable. (p. 18)

Critical Mass's principal political-social purpose is
exuberantly to reclaim the city streets for cyclists. But as
a consequence of this aim, Critical Mass inevitably halts
(motorised) traffic, sometimes in ways outsiders see as anarchic civil disobedience (indeed resulting in 'fallout' in the
form of arrests and violent attacks on cyclists). A second
consequence is that the movement challenges the economies
and behaviours that motorised traffic supports, from the felt
'need' to earn enough at work to buy a car to drive there,
to road rage, to pollution, to wealthy nations' deep fiscal
and political investment in oil and the wars it has motivated.
Although we might see Critical Mass as having theatrical
elements – cyclists often wear costumes, for example – the
point I want to emphasise is that it is performative; doing it
effects change. During the rides, the change is material; the
cyclists take over the streets. But even outside the scheduled
rides, Critical Mass hopes to have an effect, through changing what we might call, after Butler, the *stylized repetition
of acts*' of behaviour in urban space.

Highly visible performative intervention:
Reverend Billy and the Church of Stop Shopping face
the Shopocalypse

New York-based performance artist William Talen has performed as his alter ego Reverend Billy of the Church of Stop

Shopping since the mid-1990s. As Jill Lane observes in her eponymous article on Reverend Billy (2002), he uses 'abominating semi-ironic preaching' to 'rag[e] against the noxious effects of consumerism, transnational capital, and the privatization of public space and culture in New York City' (p. 60). His oratory in part satirises televangelism and the complicity of right-wing Christianity's connections to supposedly free market values, but it also addresses – and performatively produces – a community and a spirit of social activism. He sometimes performs in theatre venues such as the Salon Theatre (subsequently 45 Bleecker Street) and St Clements Church, but he is best known for his on-street and in-shop sermons, services and interventions outside or inside a Disney Store or various Manhattan Starbucks, where he argues that an apparently benign cup of coffee or toy is actually part of a long chain of exploitative production practices or a blissful narrative that nevertheless reifies oppressive representations.

Like the practices referred to earlier in this section, Reverend Billy's work is performative in that it practises non-conventional behaviour in order to interrupt, defamiliarise and transform conventional, repetitive – and oppressive – social behaviours. By not shopping, Billy aims to stop shopping. And just as Lefebvre recognised that de-prioritising the automobile in the city might be difficult, Billy recognises that stopping shopping here might be difficult too. In *What Should I Do If Reverend Billy Is in My Store?*, he writes:

> Like crack cocaine or membership in the National
> Rifle Association, shopping is an annihilating

addiction that must be slowed down to be
stopped. Or flooded with new and different light.
But people, please – *do something*! ... The research
phase is over. How many times do we have to
hear that seven percent of the world's population
is taking a third of the world's resources? How
many neighborhoods need to be malled? When
will our foreign policy be violent enough to turn
our heads? (p. xiii)

His Cell Phone Operas famously exploit mobile technologies in a new twist on Augusto Boal's invisible theatre
actions (see Boal's *Games for Actors and Non-Actors*, 1992)
and an inversion of what Williams warned was the pro-
pensity of 'mobile privatisation' to effect social separation
and isolation. Billy's Operas are a form of 'flash mob' – the
rapid mobilisation using email and cell phones of a group
of protestors to enact a brief performative protest, such as
dancing in the street, designed to collectivise and protest
against socially imposed pressures the organisers see as limiting, such as the urban instruction to shop, shop, shop. In a
chapter describing 'retail interventions' in *What Would Jesus
Buy?* (2006), Talen outlines 'Cell Phone Opera Number
One':

> *Works well with between fifteen and twenty-five church
> members. Enter the store in character as single shop-
> pers. The Church members pretend not to know each
> other, but everyone has essentially the SAME story.*

Each of you has been sent by a wife or husband on an errand: to go to this store and buy something for a child's birthday.

One by one you get on your cell phones to object to the choice of gift. ... Make up some refusenik-style theater: 'Do you think Cindy should idolize this Snow White doll? The little wasp waist, c'mon!' (pp. 40–1; italics original)

The aim is 'that the social conscience of our innocent browser can be excited' (p. 41): the live demonstration of not-shopping makes the non-self-reflexive shopper suddenly self-reflexive; the would-be shopper recognises his or her complicity in – in this example – the reification of sexist ideologies; the 'innocent browser' retreats from the brink and does not shop.

Like the situationists, Billy works in and with the streets and shops, intervening in apparently everyday behaviours in everyday sites of commoditisation, exploitation and gentrification. He also crucially deploys humour to engage his church members as well as unsuspecting observers and to challenge the corporate formality which aims to discredit him and which, therefore, masks corporate violence. Billy's book *What Should I Do If Reverend Billy Is in My Store?* takes its title from an internal Starbucks memo (reproduced at the front of the book) which soberly informs Starbucks staff to ask Reverend Billy to leave and, if he fails to do so, to page district managers and marketing personnel and call the police. In an extension of the situationists' focus, Billy draws particular attention to how sites of apparent leisure and play – which we reasonably expect to be the opposite of (exploitative) work – are actually deeply caught up in some rather ruthless practices, rhetorics and ideologies of capitalist exploitation and commoditisation.

A performative right to the city

There is much about a critical approach focusing on performativity as outlined in this section that is not only optimistic about the possibility of positive, liberating urban social change but also demonstrates practical strategies to effect that change. And there are numerous other examples of performative urban cultural practices I could discuss, including guerrilla gardening, communications and culture jamming, anarchic circus and clowning, graffiti, skateboarding and *parkour*, or free running. (For further examples, see Notes from Nowhere, *We Are Everywhere*, 2003.) Most important, across its huge range of practices, this performative critical approach credits people as social agents, individuals with the freedom and ability to act performatively to change our lives, destinies and urban society in an age of global capitalism. In this section, we have seen especially how performative practices are used to advocate for renewed urban practices that challenge the spatial hegemony of social isolation in motorised vehicles and the social hegemony of work, capitalist alienation and consumerism. We have seen performative practices claim the right to the city for a more democratic demographic and an extended set of activities, including not only working and consuming but also – or instead – feeling and 'unproductive' play.

However, as with cultural materialist critical practice, there are again drawbacks to performative analysis in this context. Crucially, we could see this critical practice as *overly* optimistic, even naive, in both its choice of object and its contextualisation of that object. *Most* performative analysis of urban cultural practices focuses on those which resist hegemonic oppression, practices such as cycling, feeling, wandering 'unproductively' and not shopping. Implicitly, however, this focus recognises the hegemony of cultural practices such as driving a car, quantifying, efficiently travelling to work and shopping. Although performative analysis has been used to examine the production of hegemony – as discussed above, through state ceremonies, conventional gender practices, family structures, understandings of etiquette, and so on – work of this kind is comparatively scarce, suggesting a wilful optimism in critics' choice of focus. I unapologetically include myself in this wilfully optimistic group, noting that pursuing what may appear impossible is a conscious project of much of this critical practice. As the situationists put it, 'Be realistic, demand the impossible' (Knabb, ed., *Situationist International Anthology*, p. 451).

This optimism applies not only to object choice but also to context of analysis, because most performative analysis broadly assumes that, ultimately, subjects have agency, that we can do what we want, when and where we want, thereby effecting positive social change. But as the preceding section of this book, on cultural materialism, aimed to demonstrate, what we can and cannot do is profoundly conditioned – or constrained – by the material conditions in which we try to do it. As Butler herself asked rhetorically in *Bodies That Matter* (1993), 'If performativity is construed as that power of discourse to produce effects through reiteration, how are we to understand the limits of such production, the constraints under which such production occurs?' (p. 20). (Indeed, it is Butler's project in both *Gender Trouble* and *Bodies That Matter* to explore how performative practice and material experience are necessarily connected.) As Butler's point acknowledges, we may not always be able to exercise our agency or change things in ways we would like. It might indeed be *useful* to recognise how theatre and urban cultures are socially oppressive rather than wishfully to think they are inevitably sites of liberation just because we want them to be; recognising their limitations might usefully help us address those limitations.

Furthermore, it is usually the case that cultural materialist analysis is used to explore the (repressive) conditions of theatre production, whereas performative analysis is used to explore the (liberating) effects of more everyday practices or less conventional performances. One problem with this selective pairing of objects and practices is that it reproduces understandings of the theatre industry as problematically complicit with hegemonic socio-political ideologies and understandings of street performance and other performative acts as necessarily liberating. It prevents us from considering how we might seek examples of anti-hegemonic practice within 'the belly of the beast', within the theatre industry itself. And it prevents us from exploring how we might find within the apparent haven of performativity conditions of inequality and oppression, as well as how, by cultivating such a strong and reassuring sense of agency, such performance practices may actually be more *insidiously* apolitical or depoliticising than performance which is more obviously conventional or commercial. These separations of objects and analyses also reinforce disciplinary separations between theatre studies and performance studies, impoverishing both.

Thus, the project of the final part of this book is to begin to explore how we might think these two critical strategies – cultural materialist and performative analyses – and these two sets of objects – theatre industries and performative practices – together so that we can best understand the complex relationships between theatre, performance and the city in an age of global capitalism. What happens, I ask, if we hybridise these critical practices and the objects they are usually applied to? But, first, a little more on why we should do this.

Conclusions: city, theatre, performance, hybridity, ambivalence and cosmopolitanism

We need to hybridise cultural materialist and performative analytic strategies, and use them to think across theatre and performance practices together, for at least three reasons. First, such an approach redistributes some of cultural materialism's caution and performativity's hope, avoiding the impasses of being too pessimistic or too optimistic. Second, theatre and performance practices are, after all, part of the same, concurrent cultural economy and ecology: New York City's vast theatre/performance culture encompasses Broadway and Reverend Billy; London's, the West End and *Rider Spoke*. It is tempting – and, in many ways, critically productive – to think separately about these two areas of practice. But, by separating them, we may reinforce a tension between them rather than address it. Thinking about theatre and performance together, about how they relate to and negotiate one another, and about the material conditions and performative practices of both in a symbiotic economy/ecology – all this should help us understand their cultural effects as part of contemporary urban social experience better and in greater complexity.

And this aspect of complexity is the third reason I propose this hybrid approach. We need an analytic strategy that has some complexity to understand the complex cultural effects of contemporary urban life. What is so complex about contemporary urban life, I would argue, is the sense of profound ambivalence it creates. Ambivalence is, of course, the sense of having at least two – usually contrasting – feelings about the same thing. The story told by this book so far is one of ambivalence: we have seen how the material conditions of theatre in the city seem to deprive us of social and material opportunities *and* how the performative practices of everyday life in the city seem to provide us with social opportunities to change, among other things, our material opportunities. We might certainly feel ambivalent, therefore, about the relationships of the theatre, performance and the city to social opportunity or, as we might otherwise name it, democracy.

And contemporary urban experience provokes a sense of ambivalence in many other ways – in relation to production and consumption, the local and the global, energy consumption and climate change, spectacle and surveillance, and danger and security, to name but a few. In our socio-economic age of quickly expanding post-industrialisation in the West and North and of rapid industrialisation in the East and South, it can be difficult to pin down the precise routes of capital's circulation, the sites of labour, who performs it, and under what conditions, and the links of responsibility between different parts of the dispersed chain of cultural production and consumption. Our experience of our cities is also, ambivalently, both local and global in an age of cosmopolitanism (a term I return to). Our city is local when we act locally – for example, cycling in Critical Mass – and when we share (everyday) experiences with our neighbours – in the street or at the theatre. It is global when we recognise how it is linked beyond its borders: our neighbours may be immigrants, as we ourselves might be; we hear many languages on its streets; we buy things here from far away – including tickets to international theatre events. In a 1991 article, geographer Doreen Massey has famously called this sense of the global in the local 'a global sense of place'. Attitudes to travel between global cities also may be ambivalent: some people are experiencing historically unprecedented opportunities to travel globally and learn firsthand about other cities and cultures; at the

71

same time, the ecological impact of global travel risks damaging the fragile globe we are keen to see. We might experience Debord's society of spectacle ambivalently too, as both pleasurable when it brings us spectacular theatre and menacing when it threatens to commoditise our cultures, or when it subjects us to excessive surveillance. And of course, cities are ambivalently places of danger and security, as demonstrated so vividly when they are sites of terrorist attacks, immediately after which strangers rush to help one another, as in Manhattan on 11 September 2001 and in London on 7 July 2005. Experiences in the city are not only multiple but also, as the above examples indicate, ambivalent, even contradictory. We need to attempt to think our critical practices together to account for these qualities and understand them as best we can.

Hybrid critical practices: materialist performativity and performative materialism

What would the hybrid critical practices I am proposing do and look like? For one thing, they might address in more detail the material conditions of performative practices and the performative effects of the material theatre.

What might be the benefits of a materialist performativity? Most important, it would examine the material conditions in which performative practices take place and the limits those conditions produce for entirely free participation and therefore for everyone's hoped-for self-realisation. We might consider how *Rider Spoke*'s celebration of self-directed personal liberty in the city depends nevertheless on the material conditions of serious money and advanced technology – dozens of bicycles and mini-computers and the capital required to provide them, supported by Blast Theory's host, that major cultural institution, the Barbican Centre, itself supported by the City of London, London's central financial district. We might also try to assess the economic impact of Reverend Billy's interventions, whether the sense of agency they engender may be more apparent than real, and the possibility that onlookers might see Billy as part of Times Square's many pleasurable spectacles rather than as a challenge to them. A materialist performative analysis might thus work to qualify some of performative analysis's more utopian claims, to show how they are certainly conditioned and likely constrained – if not entirely cancelled out – by capital and other materialities. The mission of this approach would not be wantonly to destroy performativity's utopianism but to suggest how performative analysis's claims might be more carefully qualified.

How might a performative materialism work? Instead of seeing the theatre industry's material conditions as inevitably constraining, we might see them as, indeed, performative and consider how they can positively change theatre and urban life. One context where we might think about the performative practices of theatre is in connection with energy use and climate change. The conventional theatre industry is a gluttonous energy consumer. I referred above to the number of articulated lorries it reportedly takes to transfer a touring *Phantom of the Opera*: twenty-seven. But even much less ostentatious non-touring theatre consumes enormous amounts of materials, space and energy, for both 'climate control' and lighting. Performatively and materially, the conventional theatre is ecologically damaging.

However, there is a growing trend to address this industrial problem, and not just through plays about climate change. In its Arcola Energy project, launched in July 2007, East London's Arcola Theatre committed itself to becoming, in the words of its launch brochure, 'the world's first carbon neutral theatre' (p. 4). It proposes to knock an initial eighteen tonnes per annum off its carbon dioxide emissions by completing a '[b]aseline refurbishment including double glazing all windows, draught proofing the building, and fitting it with a controlled ventilation system' (p. 6). The theatre will then eliminate its net carbon dioxide emissions of fifty-four tonnes per annum through more sensible energy use and the introduction of renewable heating and electricity. Finally, the project will spread good ecological practice through leadership and training, as well as through demonstrating to its theatre-making community and audiences an ecologically sound theatre practice that does not compromise its artistic product. Other theatres too are making some if not all of these types of ecological change. On 22 October 2007, London's then-mayor Ken Livingstone announced in a press release that he was working in partnership with London theatres and their organisations – including Arts Council England's London office, the Theatres Trust, the Ambassador Theatre Group, the Independent Theatre Council and Equity – to reduce London theatre's carbon emissions and to produce a Climate Change Action Plan for London Theatre. On the same day, the National Theatre in London announced the start of a five-year scheme with Royal Philips Electronics to replace the theatre's lighting. Not only was this initiative ecological; it was aesthetic: Philips proudly pointed out in its press release that the use of energy-efficient LED lights to illuminate the exterior of the National Theatre's flytowers would give it 'an endless colour palette with which to paint the building'.

Admittedly, the example of Arcola Energy might seem somewhat extraordinary and – at a cost in capital expenditure of between £250,000 and £350,000 – beyond the means of most theatre companies. But we can also think about more ordinary, everyday ways in which theatre performatively enacts some positive social configuration – for example, when a theatre draws an audience that feels like a community. This is the specific project of thousands of global community-based theatre and performance organisations that aim to effect social change, including the many described in Susan C. Haedicke and Tobin Nellhaus' collection *Performing Democracy* (2001). But a sense of community might also be produced in theatres whose work is not explicitly about social action – for example, theatres for local communities, such as northwest London's Tricycle Theatre, which aims specifically to address local black and Irish communities, or the Theatre Royal, Stratford East, which aims to address local black and Asian audiences. Of course, the production of a sense of community may not be a wholly good thing – it may be exclusive or coercive. But it can work for positive social change, especially where that community is not predominantly catered for by mainstream theatre or is socially disadvantaged.

A cosmopolitan community

But it is also possible to have that extraordinary (ordinary) performative experience of feeling like a community in an audience one feels very different among – the people look older than me, or younger, or are from a different class, area, ethnicity or nation, or are simply all strangers to me. What is exciting about this kind of experience is, for me, the profound, almost visceral recognition that I share a feeling with an audience who otherwise feel different; in other words, that I feel my simultaneous similarity and difference within that audience. And understanding this ambivalence might be aided not by trying to reconcile our critical approaches to theatre and the city but by acknowledging the tensions within and between them.

For some theorists, the experience I have just described is both the challenge and the opportunity of the contemporary urban experience of cosmopolitanism; it requires us to recognise our shared, even universal, characteristics with our fellow humans globally, at the same time as we respect each other's legitimate differences. This is a challenge both because it requires us to sympathise with literally billions of people whom we will never, ever meet and because it asks us to respect others' legitimate differences, even though it may be difficult for us to understand them. It is an opportunity because our lives are necessarily globally connected, both in the multicultural cities we live in and among our distantly located but connected cities. In his book, *Cosmopolitanism* (2005), Kwame Anthony Appiah explains that the Cynics of the fourth century BCE coined the term 'cosmopolitan' to identify a 'citizen of the cosmos', rather than merely of one's own civic locality: 'The formulation was meant to be paradoxical, and reflected the general Cynic skepticism toward custom and tradition. A citizen – a *politēs* – belonged to a particular *polis*, a city to which he or she owed loyalty. The cosmos referred to the world, not in the sense of the earth, but in the sense of the universe' (p. xiv). The term therefore articulates an ethical need to 'understand those with whom we share the planet', especially in economic terms (p. xv). Appiah acknowledges that 'there will be times when these two ideals – universal concern and respect for legitimate difference – clash' (p. xv). So he proposes that rather than seeing a state of cosmopolitanism as already achieved, we consider it a goal, a challenge to be pursued through 'habits of coexistence: conversation in its older meaning, of living together, association' (p. xix).

Being a theatre or performance audience or maker, deliberately and performatively gathering in the same time and material space as other people to share a cultural experience, can be, in this way, an affirmative act of conversation and cosmopolitanism, an opportunity ambivalently to respect our differences and recognise what we share, to recognise the challenges we live with in our cities and to take up cities' opportunities. Theatre and performance in the contemporary urban context certainly face challenges in offering both practices and visions of a better world, but they also offer hope, in part because, as this book has sought to demonstrate, they are particularly well equipped to help us think about and enact both material practices and performative visions. They can help us see, for example, the conditions of economic inequality that Gary, Steve and the City executives live with in *Small Metal Objects*, but also the social possibilities of communication, understanding and change within and despite those conditions.

further reading

A great overview article on theatre, performance and the city in contemporary culture is Garner's. Most writing on the city's representation in drama focuses on the early modern period, for example the collection edited by Smith *et al.* and Dillon's *Theatre, Court and City, 1596–1610*. Lehan's *The City in Literature* focuses on fiction, but its critical approaches might be adapted to analyse drama. Key writers who adopt a predominantly cultural material-ist approach to the theatre and the city are Carlson, Davis, McKinnie, Kershaw and Knowles; this approach is shared by *Theatre Journal*'s 2001 special issue on 'Theatre and the City'. Critical material underpinning this approach is repre-sented here by Dollimore and Sinfield, Marx and Williams. Important texts addressing performance's urban performa-tivity include those edited by Cohen-Cruz, Hopkins *et al.*, McAuley and Sandford and those by Kaprow, Kirby, Pearson and Shanks, Talen and Wickstrom. Criticism which explores broader ideas of performativity is represented here by Austin, Benjamin, Butler, Debord, De Certeau, Lefebvre and the collection edited by Knabb. Critical reading in cultural studies and social geography which underpins the arguments of my approach is by Appiah, Bennett, Harvey, Massey, and Miles and Hall with Borden.

Alÿs, Francis. *Francis Alÿs: Seven Walks: London, 2004–5*. London: Artangel, 2005.

Appiah, Kwame Anthony. *Cosmopolitanism: Ethics in a World of Strangers*. London: Allen Lane (Penguin), 2006.

Arcola Energy. 'Arcola Energy Brochure.' London, July 2007. July 2008 <www.arcolaenergy.com>.

Aristophanes. *The Birds and Other Plays*. London: Penguin, 2003.

Austin, J. L. *How To Do Things with Words*. 2nd ed. Ed. J. O. Urmson and Marina Sbisa. Oxford: Clarendon Press, 1975.

Benjamin, Walter. *The Arcades Project*. Cambridge, MA: Harvard UP, 2002.

Bennett, Susan. *Theatre Audiences: A Theory of Production and Reception*. 2nd ed. London and New York: Routledge, 1997.

Boal, Augusto. *Games for Actors and Non-Actors*. Trans. Adrian Jackson. London and New York: Routledge, 1992.

Butler, Judith. *Bodies That Matter: On the Discursive Limits of 'Sex'*. New York and London: Routledge, 1993.

———. *Gender Trouble: Feminism and the Subversion of Identity*. 2nd ed. New York and London: Routledge, 1999.

Carlson, Marvin. *Places of Performance: The Semiotics of Theatre Architecture*. Ithaca, NY, and London: Cornell UP, 1989.

Carlsson, Chris, ed. *Critical Mass: Bicycling's Defiant Celebration*. Edinburgh, London and Oakland, CA: AK Press, 2002.

Churchill, Caryl. *Serious Money*. *Plays: Two*. London: Methuen, 1990. 193–309.

Clarke, John. 'Capitalism.' *New Keywords: A Revised Vocabulary of Culture and Society*. Ed. Tony Bennett, Lawrence Grossberg and Meaghan Morris. Oxford: Blackwell, 2005. 22–6.

Cohen-Cruz, Jan, ed. *Radical Street Performance: An International Anthology*. London and New York: Routledge, 1998.

Cook, Deborah. *The Culture Industry Revisited: Theodor W. Adorno on Mass Culture*. Lanham, MD: Rowman & Littlefield, 1996.

Davidson, Clifford. 'The York Cycle.' *International Dictionary of Theatre*, vol. 1: *Plays*. Ed. Mark Hawkins-Dady. Chicago and London: St James Press, 1992. 924–7.

Davis, Tracy C. *Actresses as Working Women: Their Social Identity in Victorian Culture*. London and New York: Routledge, 1991.

————. *The Economics of the British Stage, 1800–1914*. Cambridge: Cambridge UP, 2000.

Debord, Guy. *The Society of the Spectacle*. 1967. Trans. Donald Nicholson-Smith. New York: Zone, 1994.

De Certeau, Michel. *The Practice of Everyday Life*, vol. 1. Trans. S. Rendall. Berkeley: U of California P, 1984.

Dillon, Janette. *Theatre, Court and City, 1595–1610: Drama and Social Space in London*. Cambridge, Cambridge UP, 2000.

Dollimore, Jonathan, and Alan Sinfield. Foreword: Cultural Materialism. *The Shakespeare Myth*. Ed. Graham Holderness. Manchester: Manchester UP, 1988.

Finlay, Roger, and Beatrice Shearer. 'Population Growth and Suburban Expansion.' *London 1500–1700: The Making of the Metropolis*. Ed. A. L. Beier and Roger Finlay. London: Longman, 1986.

Garner, Stanton B., Jr. 'Urban Landscapes, Theatrical Encounters: Staging the City.' *Land/Scape/Theater*. Ed. Elinor Fuchs and Una Chaudhuri. Ann Arbor: U of Michigan P, 2002. 94–118.

Greater London Authority. *London Divided: Income Inequality and Poverty in the Capital*. London, Nov. 2002. Oct. 2008 <www.london.gov. uk/mayor/economy/docs/london_divided_all.pdf>.

Haedicke, Susan C., and Tobin Nellhaus, eds. *Performing Democracy: International Perspectives on Urban Community-Based Performance*. Michigan: U of Michigan P, 2001.

Harris, John Wesley. 'Medieval Theatre in Europe.' *The Oxford Encyclopedia of Theatre & Performance*, vol 2. Ed. Dennis Kennedy. Oxford: Oxford UP, 2003. 824–37.

Harvey, David. *The Urban Experience*. Oxford: Blackwell, 1989.

Harvie, Jen. *Staging the UK*. Manchester: Manchester UP, 2005.

Henderson, Mary C. *The City and the Theatre: The History of New York Playhouses: A 250 Year Journey from Bowling Green to Times Square*. New York: Back Stage, 2004.

Hopkins, D. J., Kim Solga, and Shelley Orr, eds. *Performance and the City*. Houndmills, UK: Palgrave, 2009.

Jonson, Ben. *Bartholmew Fair*. Introduction by Alexander Leggatt. Ed. G. R. Hibbard. 2nd rev. ed. London: A & C Black, 2007.

Kaprow, Allan. *Essays on the Blurring of Art and Life*. Expanded ed. Ed. Jeff Kelley. Berkeley: U of California P, 2003.

Keay, Douglas. 'Aids, Education and the Year 2000!' [interview with Margaret Thatcher]. *Women's Own*, 31 Oct. 1987. 8–10. Excerpt on the Margaret Thatcher Foundation website, Oct. 2008 <www.margaretthatcher.org/speeches/displaydocument. asp?docid=106689>.

Keith, Michael, and Steve Pile. 'Introduction Part 2: The Place of Politics.' *Place and the Politics of Identity*. Ed. Keith and Pile. London: Routledge, 1993. 22–40.

Kershaw, Baz. *The Radical in Performance: Between Brecht and Baudrillard*. London: Routledge, 1999.

———. *Theatre Ecology: Environments and Performance Events*. Cambridge: Cambridge UP, 2007.

King, Pamela M. *The York Mystery Cycle and the Worship of the City*. Westfield Medieval Studies, vol. 1. Cambridge: D.S. Brewer, 2006.

Kintz, Linda. 'Performing Capital in Caryl Churchill's *Serious Money*.' *Theatre Journal* 51.3 (1999): 251–65.

Kipling, George. 'Wonderfull Spectacles: Theatre and Civic Culture.' *A New History of Early English Drama*. Ed. John D. Cox and David Scott Kastan. New York: Columbia UP, 1997.

Kirby, Michael. *Happenings: An Illustrated Anthology*. London: Sidgwick and Jackson, 1965.

Knabb, Ken, trans. and ed. *Situationist International Anthology*. Rev. and expanded ed. Berkeley, CA: Bureau of Public Secrets, 2006.

Knowles, Ric. *Reading the Material Theatre*. Cambridge: Cambridge UP, 2004.

Lane, Jill. 'Reverend Billy: Preaching, Protest, and Postindustrial Flânerie.' *The Drama Review* 46.1 (2002): 60–84.

Lefebvre, Henri. *The Urban Revolution*. 1970. Trans. Robert Bononno. Minneapolis and London: U of Minnesota P, 2003.

————. *Writings on Cities*. Trans. and ed. Eleonore Kofman and Elizabeth Lebas. Oxford: Blackwell, 1996.

Lehan, Richard. *The City in Literature: An Intellectual and Cultural History*. Berkeley: U of California P, 1998.

Marx, Karl. *Capital: A Critique of Political Economy*. Harmondsworth and London: Penguin and New Left Review, 1976.

Marx, Karl, and Friedrich Engels. *The Communist Manifesto: A Modern Edition*. London and New York: Verso, 1998.

Massey, Doreen. 'A Global Sense of Place.' *Marxism Today*, June 1991. 24–9.

————. *World City*. Cambridge: Polity, 2007.

Mayor of London. 'Mayor Joins with London Theatres to Make the Industry Cleaner and Greener.' Press release, London, 22 Oct. 2007. July 2008 <www.london.gov.uk/view_press_release. jsp?releaseid=14179>.

McAuley, Gay, ed. *Unstable Ground: Performance and the Politics of Place*. Brussels: Peter Lang, 2006.

McConachie, Bruce A. *Melodramatic Formations: American Theatre & Society, 1820–1870*. Iowa City: U of Iowa P, 1992.

McKinnie, Michael. *City Stages: Theatre and Urban Space in a Global City*. Toronto: U of Toronto P, 2007.

Miles, Malcolm, and Tim Hall with Iain Borden, eds. *The City Cultures Reader*. 2nd ed. London and New York: Routledge, 2004.

Morley, Sheridan. *Theatre's Strangest Acts: Extraordinary but True Tales from Theatre's Colourful History*. London: Robson, 2006.

Notes from Nowhere, ed. *We Are Everywhere: The Irresistible Rise of Global Anticapitalism*. London and New York: Verso, 2003.

Office for National Statistics, UK. 2001 Census, Key Statistics: Ethnic Group (KS06). Oct. 2008 <www.neighbourhood.statistics.gov.uk/ dissemination/LeadTableView.do?a=7&b=276767&c=Newham&d= 13&e=15&g=343478&i=1001x1003x1004&m=0&r=1&s=1223119 597194&enc=1&dsFamilyId=47>.

Orlin, Lena Cowen. Introduction. *Material London, ca. 1600*. Ed. Orlin. Philadelphia: U of Pennsylvania P, 2000. 1–13.

Pearson, Mike, and Michael Shanks. *Theatre/Archaeology*. London: Routledge, 2001.

Philips. 'National Theatre Lights Go Up.' Press release, 22 Oct. 2007. July 2008 <www.nationaltheatre.org.uk/Press20Releases%201709.twl>.

Plant, Sadie. *The Most Radical Gesture: The Situationist International in a Postmodern Age*. London and New York: Routledge, 1992.

Rebellato, Dan. *Theatre & Globalization*. London: Palgrave, 2009.

Ridout, Nicholas. *Stage Fright, Animals, and Other Theatrical Problems*. Cambridge: Cambridge UP, 2006

Román, David. *Performance in America: Contemporary U.S. Culture and the Performing Arts*. Durham, NC, and London: Duke UP, 2005.

Royal Shakespeare Company. *Annual Report and Accounts, 2007/08*. Stratford-upon-Avon, 2008. Oct. 2008 <www.rsc.org.uk/downloads/pdfs/annualreport2008.pdf>.

Sandford, Mariellen R., ed. *Happenings and Other Acts*. London and New York: Routledge, 1995.

Shadwell, Thomas. *The Volunteers, or The Stockjobbers*. London, 1693.

'Shaftesbury Avenue'. *Survey of London: volumes 31 and 32: St James Westminster, Part 2*, 1963. 68–84. Oct. 2008 <www.british-history.ac.uk/report.aspx?compid=41455>.

Smith, David L., Richard Strier, and David Bevington. *The Theatrical City: Culture, Theatre and Politics in London, 1576–1649*. Cambridge: Cambridge UP, 1995.

Soja, Edward. *Postmodern Geographies*. London: Verso, 1989.

Sophocles. *Oedipus Rex*. Ed. R. D. Dawe. 2nd ed. Cambridge: Cambridge UP, 2006.

Stock, Angela, and Anne-Julia Zwierlein. 'Introduction: "Our Scene is London …".' *Plotting Early Modern London: New Essays on Jacobean City Comedy*. Ed. Dieter Mehl, Angela Stock and Anne-Julia Zwierlein. Aldershot: Ashgate, 2004. 1–24.

Talen, William [Reverend Billy]. *What Should I Do If Reverend Billy Is in My Store?* New York and London: New Press, 2003.

———. *What Would Jesus Buy? Fabulous Prayers in the Face of the Shopocalypse*. New York: PublicAffairs, 2006.

Templeton, Fiona. *YOU – The City*. New York: Roof Books, 1990.

Theatre and the City. Ed. Susan Bennett. Spec. iss. of *Theatre Journal* 53.2 (2001).

United Nations Human Settlements Programme (UN-HABITAT). *The State of the World's Cities: Globalization and Urban Culture*. London: Earthscan, 2006.

Walkowitz, Judith R. *City of Dreadful Delight: Narratives of Sexual Danger in Late-Victorian London*. Chicago: U of Chicago P, 1992.

Welch, David. *Propaganda and the German Cinema 1933–1945*. Oxford: Clarendon Press, 1983.

Wickstrom, Maurya. *Performing Consumers: Global Capital and Its Theatrical Seductions*. London: Routledge, 2006.

Williams, Raymond. 'Culture Is Ordinary.' *Conviction*. Ed. Norman MacKenzie. London: MacGibbon & Kee, 1958. 74–92.

————. *Television: Technology and Cultural Form*. Ed. Ederyn Williams. London and New York: Routledge, 1974. Routledge Classics ed. 2003.

Websites

Back to Back Theatre Company: www.backtobacktheatre.com (accessed Oct. 2008).

Blast Theory: www.blastheory.co.uk (accessed July 2008).

Critical Mass: www.critical-mass.org (accessed July 2008).

New York City Theatre.com: www.new-amsterdam-theatre.com (accessed Oct. 2008).

Really Useful Group: www.reallyuseful.com (accessed Oct. 2008).

Templeton, Fiona: www.fionatempleton.org (accessed Aug. 2008).

index

Theatre& small books on theatre & everything else

NEW FOR 2010...

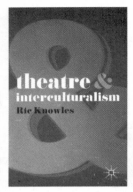

978-0-230-57548-6

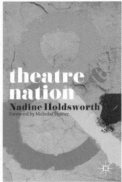

978-0-230-57462-5

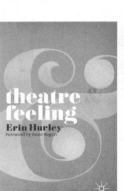

978-0-230-21846-8

978-0-230-21871-0

978-0-230-22064-5

'Palgrave Macmillan's excellent new outward-looking, eclectic *Theatre*& series. These short books, written by leading theatre academics, do much to reintroduce some of the brightest names in theatre academia to the general reader.' - Guardian Theatre blog

heatre& small books on theatre & everything else

PUBLISHED IN 2009...

978-0-230-20522-2

978-0-230-20523-9

978-0-230-20524-6

978-0-230-20543-7

'Short, sharp shots' for theatre students and enthusiasts
Presenting the best writing from A-list scholars
Vibrant and inspiring

978-0-230-21028-8

978-0-230-21830-7

978-0-230-21027-1

978-0-230-21857-4

Place your order online at www.palgrave.com